Creative Problem Solving

A Step-by-Step Approach

Robert A. Harris

Pyrczak Publishing
P.O. Box 39731 ● Los Angeles, CA 90039

Although the author and publisher have made every effort to ensure the accuracy and completeness of information contained in this book, we assume no responsibility for errors, inaccuracies, omissions, or any inconsistency herein. Any slights of people, places, or organizations are unintentional.

Project Director: Monica Lopez

Cover design by Robert Kibler and Larry Nichols based on a photograph by Larry Nichols.

Editorial assistance provided by Sharon Young, Brenda Koplin, Cheryl Alcorn, and Randall R. Bruce.

Printed in the United States of America by McNaughton and Gunn, Inc.

ISBN 1-884585-43-4

Contents

Introduction   v

Chapter 1   Creative Thinking As a Problem-Solving Tool   1
   1.1 What is creative thinking?   1
   1.2 Why is creative thinking important to problem solving?   3
   1.3 Creative problem-solving methods   6

Chapter 2   The Creative-Thinking Outlook   11
   2.1 Negative attitudes as blocks to creativity   11
   2.2 Misconceptions as blocks to creativity   14
   2.3 Inflexibility as a block to creativity   15
   2.4 Attitudes that strengthen creativity   18
   2.5 Behaviors that strengthen creativity   22

Chapter 3   Identifying Problems   25
   3.1 What is a problem?   25
   3.2 Inhibitors to effective problem solving   28
   3.3 Causation   29

Chapter 4   The Problem-Solving Cycle 1: Exploring the Problem   37
   4.1 Define the problem   37
   4.2 Articulate the assumptions   40
   4.3 Use a 360-degree approach   43

Chapter 5   The Problem-Solving Cycle 2: Establishing Goals   47
   5.1 The necessity of goals   47
   5.2 The importance of values   49
   5.3 Consider ideal goals   51
   5.4 Establish specific, practical goals   52

Chapter 6   The Problem-Solving Cycle 3: Generating Ideas   57
   6.1 Associative techniques   57
   6.2 Analytic techniques   60
   6.3 Creative questions   63
   6.4 Brainstorming   65
   6.5 Role playing   67

Chapter 7   The Problem-Solving Cycle 4: Choosing the Solution   71
   7.1 What is a solution?   71
   7.2 Stop-it solutions   72
   7.3 Mop-it solutions   73
   7.4 Solution paths   75
   7.5 Consequence analysis   76
   7.6 Selection   79

Chapter 8   The Problem-Solving Cycle 5: Implementing the Solution   83
   8.1 Acceptance and the management of change   83
   8.2 Solution implementation plans   87

Chapter 9   The Problem-Solving Cycle 6: Evaluating the Solution   91
   9.1 Analyze the implementation   91
   9.2 Determine needed changes   93
   9.3 Review the problem environment   95

Appendix A   Creative Thinking Activities   97
   A.1 Uses for   97
   A.2 Improvements to   98
   A.3 What is it?   99
   A.4 Writing captions   100
   A.5 What iffing   101

Appendix B   Brainstorming Activities   103
   B.1 New names   103
   B.2 Empty the glass   103
   B.3 No counterfeits   103

Appendix C   Problem-Solving Activities   104
   C.1 Analyzing a solution   104
   C.2 A familiar problem   104
   C.3 Many solutions   104

References   105

Index   106

Introduction

This book will help you sharpen the skills you need to solve unstructured problems—problems that require a thoughtful and creative approach. Structured problems such as X + 2 = 4 can be solved by learning the appropriate steps. However, unstructured problems such as how to increase revenue in a struggling bookstore must first be explored and defined. Then their solutions must be constructed through a combination of imagination and analysis.

The skills you learn in this book will help you throughout your academic career as you tackle problems such as research projects, case studies, and experiments, and as you seek to understand the material in courses such as history or sociology, which are in essence studies in human problem solving. Life is, after all, basically a problem-solving activity.

WHAT'S IN THIS BOOK?

CHAPTER 1: CREATIVE THINKING AS A PROBLEM-SOLVING TOOL.

This chapter discusses creative thinking and shows how it can be effectively used in the problem-solving process. Creative thinking methods generate the ideas that critical thinking can analyze to find solutions. Thus, creative thinking and critical thinking work as a team in the problem-solving process.

CHAPTER 2: THE CREATIVE-THINKING OUTLOOK.

This chapter explains some of the negative attitudes and misconceptions that prevent us from expressing our creativity and discusses ways to overcome them. It also covers the positive attitudes and behaviors that strengthen creative thinking and action.

CHAPTER 3: IDENTIFYING PROBLEMS.

This chapter answers these questions: What is a *problem*? What are the types? What inhibits problem solving? What is a *cause*? What kinds of causes are there? What are the common errors in analyzing causes? For a given problem, is there a single cause, a chain of causes, or a complex set of causes?

CHAPTER 4: THE PROBLEM-SOLVING CYCLE 1: EXPLORING THE PROBLEM.

This chapter covers defining and clarifying the problem, identifying (and questioning) the assumptions surrounding it, and creating multiple possible explanations for the problem as a means of understanding it better. Information about how experienced problem solvers work is also provided.

CHAPTER 5: THE PROBLEM-SOLVING CYCLE 2: ESTABLISHING GOALS.

This chapter explains how goals help to clarify the kind of solution desired and how they provide criteria for evaluating the solution. The important role of values in problem solving is covered, together with the benefit of establishing ideal goals in advance of practical goals.

CHAPTER 6: THE PROBLEM-SOLVING CYCLE 3: GENERATING IDEAS.

This chapter describes how to generate ideas. It begins with a discussion of associative techniques, including the use of analogy; it then covers analytic techniques, such as attribute analysis, and concludes with imaginative techniques of creative questions, brainstorming, and role playing.

CHAPTER 7: THE PROBLEM-SOLVING CYCLE 4: CHOOSING THE SOLUTION.

This chapter presents the information needed to choose one or more of the possible solutions generated in the previous step. Consideration is given to solution approaches, solution paths, consequence analysis, and the refinement of the solution.

CHAPTER 8: THE PROBLEM-SOLVING CYCLE 5: IMPLEMENTING THE SOLUTION.

This chapter stresses the importance of acceptance in the implementation of any solution. That is, a solution must be accepted by all those involved or it is unlikely to work well, if at all. Also covered are design and types of implementation plans and the use of timelines for the efficient accomplishment of work.

CHAPTER 9: THE PROBLEM-SOLVING CYCLE 6: EVALUATING THE SOLUTION.

This chapter explains how to evaluate the solution that has been implemented. Implementation analysis involves determining whether or not the solution worked, how well it worked, what changes are needed, and even a final look at the problem itself.

APPENDIX A: CREATIVE THINKING ACTIVITIES.

The activities here will help you form the habit of generating many ideas and alternatives, which will create a flexible mind. The activities focus on developing ideas and an imaginative, inventive outlook.

APPENDIX B: BRAINSTORMING ACTIVITIES.

This appendix supplies topics for group or individual brainstorming sessions, so that you can practice the techniques presented in Chapter 6.

APPENDIX C: PROBLEM-SOLVING ACTIVITIES.

These activities ask you to explore the solutions to problems represented by the objects of the world around you and by your own experience. The goal of the appendix is to help you transfer your newly gained textbook knowledge into practical habits.

ACKNOWLEDGMENTS.

Thanks to Fred Pyrczak for his support, ideas, and helpful comments on the drafts. Thanks to Cheryl Alcorn and Valerie Chung for their careful readings of the manuscript and for testing the chapter questions.

Robert A. Harris
Tustin, California

Chapter 1

❖

Creative Thinking As a Problem-Solving Tool

Creativity is . . . shaking hands with the future.
—E. Paul Torrance

*When I examine myself and my methods of thought, I come to
the conclusion that the gift of fantasy has meant more to me than
my talent for absorbing positive knowledge.*
—Albert Einstein

If it is true that "life is just one problem after another," then it makes sense for all of us to develop a strong problem-solving ability. The more tools we have for solving problems, the better off we and those around us will be. This chapter introduces the concept of creative thinking and explains its relationship to problem solving. The chapter explores these ideas:

- Creative thinking is a way of thinking and behaving that can be learned.
- Problem solving requires the use of a flexible and fertile imagination.
- Creative thinking employs several standard methods for generating the useful novelty that is its hallmark.

1.1 WHAT IS CREATIVE THINKING?

Many misconceptions surround the idea of creative thinking. When challenged to find a creative solution to a problem, some people respond by saying, "Well, I'm just not creative." Others say that creativity is the realm of the uniquely talented genius, born to create, and that no amount of training or effort will help the untalented. A few people even claim that creative thinking is not only impractical but irrational, having nothing to do with the "hard facts of a workaday world."

1.1.1 CREATIVE THINKING IS AN ATTITUDE.

One of the most significant attributes of creative thinkers is how they respond to problems and ideas. Creative thinkers have learned to take the time to play with all kinds of new ideas and to experiment with possibilities before focusing on a final approach. Ideas are allowed to develop and flex their wings

1

before being evaluated. Creative thinkers accept change, are comfortable with uncertainty and risk, welcome newness, and view problems as opportunities rather than as threats. If this description does not sound like you, take heart: This flexibility of outlook can be practiced and developed in anyone. (See Chapter 2, Section 2.4, for further discussion of the creative thinking mindset.)

1.1.2 CREATIVE THINKING IS A SKILL.

Yes, there are highly talented, creative artists who have inborn (and well trained) aptitudes. At the same time, being creative and applying creative thinking approaches to solving problems are learnable skills. Many techniques that will help to train your thinking to be highly creative have been developed. As with any skill, the more you practice these techniques, the more powerful a creative thinker you can become. Much of creativity involves combining, changing, or reapplying existing ideas, and the techniques presented in this book for working with ideas will enable you to perform these activities better. Some creative ideas are quite new, and the techniques for generating ideas and new solutions will strengthen your ability in this area as well.

1.1.3 CREATIVE THINKING IS A PROCESS.

Contrary to the popular misconceptions surrounding creativity, very few works of creative excellence are produced in a single attempt, and very few difficult problems are solved in a moment of unprepared insight. Note the use of the word *unprepared* here. Creative people, especially creative problem solvers, engage in many hours of research, thinking, and experimenting before beginning to develop a solution (which may indeed have come, at last, in a flash of insight). Even then, the ideas usually require shaping and refining before they are ready. As you will read again later on, persistence is one of the key qualities necessary for successful problem solving.

1.1.4 CREATIVE THINKING IS BOTH FANCIFUL AND PRACTICAL.

The charge that creative thinking is impractical, unrealistic, or foolish is sometimes made by those who have an incomplete understanding of the process and its purpose. Creative thinking involves free-flowing ideas without regard to their immediate practicality, but ultimately it concludes with an analysis and selection of ideas based on their usefulness. Another way to describe this is through the following Key of Wisdom:

Creative thinking is a journey through the imagination to a better reality.

Creative thinking begins with a reality that needs improving (this reality is known as a *problem*), and the process ends with a reality that represents an improvement over the previous one (the *goal state*). The process is therefore ultimately practical and useful. A creative solution is often described as one that is both new and useful. The creation of novelty requires imagination, while the determination of usefulness requires critical analysis.

1.2 WHY IS CREATIVE THINKING IMPORTANT TO PROBLEM SOLVING?

If the solution to every problem were obvious, problems would not last more than a few seconds. If the solution to every problem could be reached by following a straightforward formula, problems could all be assigned to computers. Problems persist because their solutions are not obvious: An approach, a thinking style, some ideas—something out of the ordinary—must be used.

1.2.1 SOLVING A PROBLEM REQUIRES IMAGINATION.

Before the techniques of critical thinking can be brought to bear on a problem, the problem itself must often be defined and structured. Unstructured problems often arrive as jumbled masses of facts. The problem solver must answer several questions in order to make sense of the situation:

- ♦ Which facts are relevant and which are irrelevant?
- ♦ What explanation could account for the facts?
- ♦ Are there alternative explanations that could account for the facts? If so, which explanation is the most probable?

In other words, the problem solver must use the facts to tell a story that includes and explains as many of the facts as possible. Only then can the story and the interrelationship of the facts be examined coherently. Many areas of problem solving require stories to structure them. Here are just a few:

- ♦ automobile troubleshooting
- ♦ medical diagnosis
- ♦ accident investigation
- ♦ crime scene analysis

Such storytelling requires an imaginative sorting and arranging of information. The following example clarifies this.

Example 1.2.1.1

A dog owner left his young puppy locked in a pen in the bedroom and went to work. Upon returning from work, the owner noted the following facts:

- ♦ The puppy was out of the pen.
- ♦ The pen was still locked.
- ♦ The puppy was running around the house excitedly.
- ♦ There were wet, yellow spots all around the outside of the pen.
- ♦ A cup on a table that had been half-full of coffee was now empty.
- ♦ The cup was near a chair that the puppy had jumped up on in the past.

♦ The puppy's water container had splashed water around it.

The owner assembled these clues into the following story: The puppy became anxious about being left alone and climbed up on the water container, which was high enough to allow the puppy to jump out of the pen. The puppy found the coffee and drank it. When the puppy had to relieve itself, it could not get back inside the pen, but was well intentioned in that it wet as near to its potty as it could get.

Note that the owner did not witness any of the events of the story, but he imaginatively constructed the most likely explanation that included all the facts. (As a result of this reconstruction, the owner moved the position of the water container so that it could not be used as a step for jumping out. He also became more careful about leaving around half-empty cups of coffee.)

1.2.2 SOLVING PROBLEMS OFTEN REQUIRES CHANGING DIRECTION.

When a problem resists a straightforward solution, creative thinking is crucial for the purpose of looking at the situation in a new way. A leap of imagination or creative insight is required.

Example 1.2.2.1

In a semirural area, the highway department lined a drainage ditch with concrete to prevent erosion of the soil. The ditch was such a smooth U-shape that soon it attracted skateboarders, who loved rolling up and down the sides. Because the skateboarding presented the danger of an accident (and a lawsuit), the highway department put up a fence to keep the kids out; the kids went around the fence. The department put up a longer fence; the kids cut a hole in it. The department put up a fence with thicker wire; the kids cut a hole in that one, too. The department then placed a threatening sign on the fence, prohibiting both skateboarding and cutting the fence. The sign was ignored on both counts.

You can see that each of these failed solutions is actually the same solution being tried again after some alteration. The view of the problem remained the same, namely, how to keep skateboarders out of the ditch, and the solution also remained the same: Build a fence. The thinking seems to have been, "When X doesn't work, what you need is a whole lot more X." However, here (as is often the case), a whole lot more X did not work, either. The problem was ultimately solved instantly, cheaply, and permanently through creative thinking, as the continued narrative below reveals.

Example 1.2.2.1, continued

Finally, someone in the highway department thought that instead of focusing on how to keep skateboarders away from an attractive skating spot, the problem solvers should change direction and focus on how to make the skating spot unappealing to the skateboarders, so that they would voluntarily stay away. The solution was to pour a few inches of concrete into the bottom of the ditch to remove the smooth curve. The sharp angle between the sides and the bottom made skateboarding down one side and up the other impossible, ending both the skateboarding problem and the fence cutting.

In this instance, some additional creative thought, some "thinking outside the box," was needed in order to solve the problem. If the problem solvers in the highway department had engaged in some brainstorming and imagining to create several possible solutions before choosing one, perhaps the better solution would have been identified at the beginning. Changing direction can take place at any time along the problem-solving process. You need not wait until you are stuck.

1.2.3 CREATIVE THINKING SUPPORTS CRITICAL THINKING.

One of the most important goals of education is that students learn how to think critically—to be able to reason closely, analyze ideas, and make good judgments. You have been learning these processes throughout your educational career because critical thinking is an essential skill for good problem solving, and problem solving describes much of life's activity. However, as you have seen above, creative thinking is an essential part of good problem solving as well. While critical thinking focuses on step-by-step, linear processes aimed at arriving at a correct answer, creative thinking begins with possibility, multiple ideas, and suspended judgment. It might be said that *creative thinking creates the ideas with which critical thinking works.*

Thus, even though these two kinds of thinking work in different ways, they actually support each other and aim at the same ultimate goal, which is to solve a problem. A useful model of an effective thinking process is that of a diamond, as seen below.

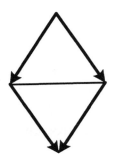

Creative diffusion phase: exploring ideas and possibilities

Critical focus phase: analyzing and selecting ideas

At the beginning of the process, creative methods are used to examine the problem environment, generate ideas, and make associations. Then the analysis and judgment faculties are brought into play, and the possibilities are analyzed for a probable solution.

1.3 CREATIVE PROBLEM-SOLVING METHODS.

A popular myth about creativity is that inventions and solutions to problems are created out of nothing—that some exceptionally gifted person sits down at a desk with a clean sheet of paper and suddenly invents the fax machine or a solution to counterfeiting. The reality is that creative problem solving is a methodical, though imaginative, process. Below are four methods that creative thinkers use to generate creative solutions.

1.3.1 REAPPLICATION.

Reapplication is the method of taking an existing item or idea and applying it to something else. The key question here is, "What else can this be used for?" Many people practice reapplication in an informal way when faced with a simple household problem. For example, a hair dryer can be used to melt candle wax off a table, and fingernail polish can be used as a kind of glue to prevent screws from loosening on machinery.

On a commercial level, many inventions have found extended use through reapplication.

Example 1.3.1.1

The magnetron tube was invented as a component of military radar stations. It was later adapted for use as the cooking element in microwave ovens.

Example 1.3.1.2

Baby food was created to serve to infants, of course. But it has been reapplied to serve to prisoners being punished in solitary confinement. Previously, serving "ten days on bread and water" was often viewed by other prisoners as a badge of honor. "Ten days on baby food," however, lacks the same sense of heroic endurance.

1.3.2 EVOLUTION.

Perhaps the most common creative method is that of evolution or gradual development, the making of incremental improvements over time. Many new ideas derive from older ideas, new solutions come by improving on previous solutions, and new inventions are indebted to the history of preceding, similar inventions. Many of the consumer products we enjoy today have been developed over time, through a process of constant change. Automobiles, telephones, clocks, refrigerators, and many other items we use daily have all been and continue to be improved regularly. The combined creativity and intelligence of many people have contributed to the development of most of the things we enjoy today. With further creativity and mental effort, those things will be even better tomorrow.

Example 1.3.2.1

The personal computer has had an explosive, though evolutionary, development. The power of the processors, the amount of memory, the capability of the software, and the reliability of the machine itself have all improved incrementally over the years. You may remember how comparatively weak computers were only a few years ago.

The evolutionary or incremental method of creative improvement has been implemented in the practice of continuous quality improvement (CQI), one of the powerful concepts at work among the best organizations today. See the box below for more information.

What Is Continuous Quality Improvement?

Continuous quality improvement (CQI) is grounded in the belief that whatever has been produced can be improved, not just once or twice, but as the term implies, continuously. A product, a manufacturing process, an interpersonal relationship, customer satisfaction, training methods—all these can be improved, regardless of how excellent they already are. In problem-solving terms, CQI follows the Key of Wisdom below.

🔑 **Every problem that has been solved can be solved again in a better way.**

The concept of improvement in CQI covers not only the addition of beneficial new features, but increases in reliability, reduction of costs, better user satisfaction, easier use, and so on. Critical to the concept, also, is the outlook of those involved in the process: They search constantly for ways to improve the things around them.

Many incremental improvements appear in the form of small refinements, while others may involve more dramatic changes.

Example 1.3.2.2

Many cars keep the same body design for several years, but even during a year between complete changeovers, there may be as many as a thousand tiny improvements to the car: an extra weld here, a rerouted wire there. Some replacement parts have been improved as well. On one model car, a replacement drain valve for the radiator had a short piece of plastic hose added to it to prevent antifreeze from splashing onto the painted surfaces of the car.

Nonphysical things, such as package delivery systems, the design of lessons for schoolchildren, and even the relationships between nations, are subject to step-by-step improvements.

Example 1.3.2.3

Years ago, bank customers would form a line at each teller's window. A customer entering the bank would look for the shortest line. The frustration was that regardless of how short the line seemed, the customer always seemed to get behind someone with lengthy business to conduct, and had to watch helplessly as all the other lines appeared to move more quickly. The solution was to form a single line, where each customer would wait for the next available teller. No one was ever stuck behind a slow transaction again.

1.3.3 SYNTHESIS.

Synthesis involves the combining of two or more ideas into a third, new idea. The ideas could be actual products, as seen in the example below.

Example 1.3.3.1

Alarm clocks work, but many people find their harsh sounds jarring and unpleasant. It would be better to be awakened by music. Combining an alarm clock and a radio resulted in the clock radio.

Or the ideas could be processes or experiences, as in the following example:

Example 1.3.3.2

Because many people on dates go to dinner first and then to the theater, why not combine the two experiences into a dinner theater? Customers first eat, perhaps with some musical entertainment, and then enjoy a play or other performance without having to get back in the car and drive somewhere else.

Sometimes concepts can be combined to suggest something new.

Example 1.3.3.3

Drivers often enjoy entertainment while commuting to and from work. They often listen to music, but what if they would like to read a magazine? The idea of reading a magazine and listening to a cassette tape or CD in the car gave rise to the idea of a magazine that commuters can listen to while they drive.

1.3.4 REVOLUTION.

The three methods described above make use of continuity in problem solving: creating something new based on previous solutions. Many times, however, the best new idea or the solution that finally works is the completely different one, a departure from previous thinking or attempts. This method makes use of discontinuity in the approach to the problem and has been described in various ways, such as *changing direction, moving to the next level,* and *taking a new ap-*

proach. Revolutionary thinking is needed when a problem remains unsolvable using the usual ideas and following the usual approaches. Example 1.2.2.1 about the fence-cutting skateboarders (see pages 4 and 5) reveals that the creative thinker often solves a problem by shifting attention from one view of the problem to another.

Example 1.3.4.1

A college student was plagued by cockroaches that entered the student's apartment from a storeroom next door. The student tried many traps, sprays, and other methods of killing the roaches, but they always came back quickly, resupplied from the storeroom. Finally, the student thought to change direction and apply a revolutionary idea. Instead of focusing on the problem, "How can I kill all the roaches?" the student asked a new question: "How can I keep the roaches out of my room?" Armed with some tubes of caulk and a caulking gun, the student sealed the area between his apartment and the storeroom and afterward enjoyed a roach-free apartment.

This example and the skateboard example earlier reveal a crucial truth about the problem-solving process: When one solution is not working, shift to another. Another Key of Wisdom tells us the same truth:

⚷ The goal is to solve the problem, not to implement a particular solution.

The problem-solver's commitment should not be to a particular path but to a particular goal. Path fixation can sometimes be a problem for those who become committed to a solution attempt that does not work; they insist on hammering away along the same path rather than looking for other possibilities. (See Chapter 7, Section 7.4, for further discussion about solution paths.) The ability to change direction, to use a revolutionary approach to solving a problem, is the mark of a strong, creative problem solver.

QUESTIONS FOR REVIEW AND DISCUSSION.

1. Comment briefly on each of the following definitions of creative thinking. Which definition do you think is the best, and why?
   (a) Creative thinking involves allowing one's imagination to run wild, without worrying about practical results.
   (b) Creative thinking is the same as problem solving.
   (c) Creative thinking combines a flexible outlook, inventive behaviors, and commitment to hard work in order to harness one's imagination in ultimately practical ways.

(d) Creative thinking involves a set of learnable techniques for working with ideas and solving problems.

2. Scientists discover the ruins of an old civilization. Hundreds of artifacts are collected. The scientists must use their imaginations before they can answer the question, "What happened here?" because they must
   A. create a story that organizes and explains the information.
   B. pretend something happened that did not.
   C. recall the plot of a novel that seems to fit the era of the civilization.

3. What is the relationship between creative and critical thinking?

4. For each of the following solutions, name the creative thinking method it best exemplifies (reapplication, evolution, synthesis, or revolution). If you think the solution fits more than one category, explain why.
   (a) A compass is built into the back of a hunting knife so that hikers need not carry a knife and compass separately.
   (b) A liquid skin salve is relabeled and sold as a mouthwash.
   (c) Numerous advances in house paint over the years make it easier to apply and more durable, with less odor and better coverage.
   (d) An electric power company uses its transmission lines to send computer data, as well as electricity, across the country.
   (e) A bookstore chain includes a coffee bar in each of its stores.
   (f) Each new version of a word processing application has more features and capability.
   (g) Doctors change their view of mental illness from a problem of child raising to a problem of brain chemistry.

5. The concept of changing direction might be described by all the following phrases **except** which one?
   A. Thinking outside the box.
   B. A leap of imagination.
   C. A revolutionary approach.
   D. Giving up on one problem and changing to another, different problem.

6. Complete the following, based on the discussion in this chapter: "_____ thinking creates the ideas with which _____ thinking works."

7. According to the text, once a problem has been solved, it
   A. is solved forever.
   B. can be solved again, but not as well.
   C. can be solved again in a better way.

Chapter 2

❖

The Creative-Thinking Outlook

We are so constituted, that if we insist upon being as sure as is
conceivable, in every step of our course, we must be content to
creep along the ground, and can never soar.
—John Henry Cardinal Newman

Genius, in truth, means little more than the faculty of perceiving
in an unhabitual way.
—William James

If creative thinking is so powerful and useful in the problem-solving process, why doesn't everybody use it all the time? This chapter examines some of the inhibiting factors or blocks to creative thinking, and then discusses the attitudes and behaviors that foster creativity.

- ◆ Creative thinking is often inhibited by negative attitudes rather than lack of ability.
- ◆ Some wrong beliefs about how problems are solved can discourage creative approaches.
- ◆ Rigid and inflexible thinking habits often interfere with the creation of imaginative solutions.
- ◆ Developing the right attitudes about creativity will strengthen your creative-thinking ability.
- ◆ Practicing creative behaviors will make you a more effective thinker.

2.1 NEGATIVE ATTITUDES AS BLOCKS TO CREATIVITY.

Life often contains many unkind experiences that teach us not to expect too much from ourselves. We have all experienced failures at some time or another, and, unfortunately, some of those failures may have given us a feeling of defeat (and that feeling may even have been reinforced by others). As a result, we may have developed some needlessly negative attitudes. Here are some of them, together with some ideas that may help counter them.

2.1.1. "PROBLEMS ARE BAD."

Those who view all problems with loathing inhibit their problem-solving ability by their unwillingness to spend time with the problems. Problems that cannot be denied or avoided are gotten rid of as quickly as possible by applying the first solution that might work. A creative approach to the problem cannot take place because no time is allowed to generate alternative ideas for solutions.

A better response to problems is to view them as opportunities. Not only will this create the environment for creative thinking, but it will allow for a happier emotional environment: The happiest people welcome and even seek out problems, meeting them as challenges and opportunities to improve things.

If you have been thinking of the problems you encounter as hateful evils, think about adopting one of these new definitions:

- A problem is an insight into the difference between what you have and what you want.
- A problem is recognizing that there is something better than the current situation.
- A problem is an opportunity for a positive act.
- A problem is a challenge to action.
- A problem is a call to creative thinking.

See Chapter 3 for further discussion about the nature of problems.

2.1.2 "I CAN'T DO IT."

A hundred years ago, many people had to do their own hunting, building, repairing, and making. Fifty years ago, many teenagers developed their skills in creative thinking and problem solving by working on old cars. Today, we are becoming more and more isolated by technology and services, so that a phenomenon known as *learned helplessness* is taking place. Now many of us feel that we do not have the skills, tools, knowledge, or materials to do anything, so we might as well not try. We are trained to rely on other people for almost everything. We think small and limit ourselves.

The truth is, you *can* do it. If you develop the ability to think creatively and add motivation, commitment, and perseverance, you can accomplish just about anything. You need not be a technical specialist.

- The Wright brothers were bicycle mechanics, not aviation engineers.
- The ballpoint pen was invented by a printer's proofreader.
- Major advances in submarine design were made by a clergyman and by a schoolmaster.
- The cotton gin was invented by that well-known attorney and tutor, Eli Whitney.
- The fire extinguisher was invented by a captain of militia.

Those who decide that they cannot solve a problem (or that the problem cannot be solved) usually fail to persevere. Another Key of Wisdom reminds us of this:

Failure to solve a problem usually means someone gave up too soon.

Of course, thinking, "I can't do it," is giving up before even starting. Many problems appear difficult or even impossible at first, but through appropriate effort and perseverance, they can be solved. The following classic example illustrates this:

Example 2.1.2.1
Take a 4-inch by 6-inch index card and make a hole in it large enough to put your head through. The card must remain in one piece.

At first glance, this problem appears to be impossible. However, there are at least half a dozen solutions to it. As you read the rest of this chapter and continue to think about creative thinking and problem solving, see how many ways you can solve this problem. Remember not to give up too soon. (Some answers are given on page 70.)

One of the myths surrounding creative thinking is that creative geniuses sit around and solve problems instantly and thoughtlessly, perhaps while they are watching television. Compared to these imaginary geniuses, it is no wonder we feel incapable. The fact is that creative thinking and problem solving are often a lot of work, even for the most creative minds.

2.1.3 "BUT I'M NOT CREATIVE."
Most of those who have this attitude believe that creativity is either inborn or impossible to possess. This attitude is both right and wrong. To some extent, creativity is indeed inborn. However, it is inborn in everyone: Everyone is creative to some extent. Most people are capable of very high levels of creativity; just look at young children when they play and use their imagination. The problem is that this creativity does not receive encouragement and training in most formal education, so that by the time students reach the university, their ability to use their creativity has diminished substantially.

For those who do not feel creative, the attitude that creativity is impossible to possess will be shown to be groundless by careful use of this book. The activities and techniques presented throughout the book are designed to help you bring your creativity back to the surface and strengthen it. You will soon discover that you are surprisingly creative.

2.1.4 "THAT'S CHILDISH."
Childish, foolish, silly, ridiculous—these are often the reactions of people who fail to understand or who believe that all solutions should be the result of an unsmiling, straight-laced process. Those who wish to appear mature and sophisticated often ridicule the creative, playful attitudes that are so prevalent among children. A six-year-old child may pretend that a cardboard box is a spaceship, but if an adult does so, people laugh critically. The fact is, though,

that the best problem solvers use play and fantasy during the problem-solving process—not just during brainstorming for new ideas, but at each stage.

Example 2.1.4.1

The stethoscope was invented by a doctor who got the idea from children playing with a stick; King Gillette was jeered at by his friends over the idea of the disposable razor; the "Fosbury flop" method of high jumping was met with laughter for its silliness—until its clear superiority made it the method of choice.

Perhaps ridicule should sometimes be viewed as a badge of really innovative thinking.

2.1.5 "I MIGHT FAIL."

Fear of failure is one of the major obstacles to creativity and problem solving. The cure is to change your attitude about failure. Failures along the way should be expected and accepted; they are simply learning tools that help focus the way toward success. Not only is there nothing wrong with failing, but failing is a sign of action and struggle and attempt—much better than inaction.

Example 2.1.5.1

Thomas Edison, in his search for the perfect filament for the incandescent lamp, tried anything he could think of, including whiskers from a friend's beard. In all, he tried about 1,800 things before succeeding. After about 1,000 attempts, someone asked him if he was frustrated by his lack of success. He replied that he had learned a lot because he now knew a thousand things that would not work.

2.2 MISCONCEPTIONS AS BLOCKS TO CREATIVITY.

We all act on the basis of our beliefs. Sometimes, though, our beliefs prevent us from acting. If we believe that nothing can be done in a given situation, we are unlikely to try anything. The following misconceptions often prevent creative thinking from occurring.

2.2.1 "EVERY PROBLEM HAS ONLY ONE SOLUTION."

The goal of problem solving is to solve the problem, and most problems can be solved in any number of ways. If you discover a solution that works, it may be a good solution, but it might not be the best one. No one would want a choice of only one kind of soap or cookies, so why not have a choice of solutions as well? Because all judgment is by comparison, the more solutions that are proposed, the easier it will be to determine which solution is the best.

Moreover, as time passes, what once was the best solution may no longer be so because advances in knowledge or technology have enabled a better one.

Example 2.2.1.1

How can words be written down? Charcoal on bark was once an excellent solution. Later we have seen the goose-quill fountain pen, ballpoint pen, pencil, printing press, marker, typewriter, dot matrix printer, inkjet printer, photocopier, and others. Now that we have color laser printers, should we stop looking for the solution?

2.2.2 "THE BEST SOLUTION HAS ALREADY BEEN FOUND."

A glance at the history of most solved problems will reveal that over time many improvements and new solutions have been adopted. Much of problem solving involves solving old problems again. See Example 2.2.1.1 above.

On a more everyday level, many solutions now entrenched were put into place hastily and without much thought—such as the use of drivers' licenses for identification cards or Social Security numbers for credit bureau tracking. Other solutions are well-established simply for historical reasons: A solution was adopted early on and has been used ever since, even as times have changed and better solutions have become possible.

2.2.3 "CREATIVE ANSWERS ARE TECHNOLOGICALLY COMPLEX."

Only a few problems require complex technological solutions. Most problems you will encounter require only a thoughtful solution needing personal action and perhaps a few simple tools. Even many problems that seem to require a technological solution can be addressed in other ways.

Example 2.2.3.1

When hot dogs were first invented, they were served to customers with gloves to hold them. Unfortunately, the customers kept walking off with the gloves. The solution was not at all complex: Serve the hot dog on a roll so that the customer's fingers were still insulated from the heat. The roll could be eaten along with the dog. No more worries about disappearing gloves. (By the way, note what a good example of changing direction this is. Instead of asking, "How can I keep the gloves from being taken?" the hot dog server stopped thinking about gloves altogether.)

2.3 INFLEXIBILITY AS A BLOCK TO CREATIVITY.

A flexible mind is one of the defining characteristics of creative thinkers. The willingness to play with ideas, change from one idea to another, associate dissimilar concepts, and think of many possibilities are all important. What is it that prevents some people from using their imaginations in a flexible way?

2.3.1 PREJUDICE.

The older we get, the more we develop preconceived ideas about what is possible. These preconceptions often prevent us from seeing beyond what we already know, and they limit our imagination. If we think that something is impossible, we certainly will not consider it as a potential solution.

Example 2.3.1.1

How can the sections of an airliner be connected with more ease and strength than by the use of rivets? A solution is to use glue—glue the sections together. We might not think of this solution because of our prejudice about the idea of *glue*. But there are many kinds of glue, and the kind used to stick plane parts together makes a bond stronger than the metal of the parts themselves. (Note that industrial glue is often called *adhesive*, in part to defuse the prejudice against the word *glue*.)

In this example, we may have developed a prejudice against glue because of our experience with it. Perhaps the glue we have used was not very good, and we have generalized about all glue from that unsuccessful use.

Example 2.3.1.2

How can a ship's hull be made so that it will not rust like steel or rot like wood? Solution: Use concrete. Our prejudice is that concrete is too heavy. Why not make lightweight concrete? Concrete-hulled ships are the result.

A chunk of concrete will definitely sink when tossed into the water, but that experience should not prevent us from imagining the use of air-filled concrete shaped into the hull of a ship. (After all, a chunk of steel will sink when tossed into the water, too, and we are not prejudiced against steel in shipbuilding.)

2.3.2 FUNCTIONAL FIXITY.

Functional fixity arises when someone is unable to see beyond the historical or accepted use for an item, often identified by its name or label. Thus, for example, a screwdriver is a tool for tightening or loosening screws, just as its name implies. A person suffering from functional fixity would be unable to see any other uses for it. But, of course, a screwdriver can also be used as a paint can opener, an ice pick, a plumb bob, a paperweight, and so on.

Similarly, to see a length of water pipe and to think of it only as a water pipe may block your thinking if you need a pry bar, a plant prop, a flagpole, a fishing rod, a measuring stick, or something else for which the pipe would work well.

Example 2.3.2.1

Several people were each given a box of candles, a box of matches, and a box of thumbtacks. They were told to discover a way to mount a candle on the wall to supply light for the room by using only those supplies. Under these circumstances, only 41 percent of the people solved the problem. (Solution: Use thumbtacks to fix a box on the wall as a platform for the candle.) However, in an experiment with other people, the candles, matches, and thumbtacks were placed outside their boxes, so that the problem-solving supplies appeared to include not only the candles, matches, and tacks, but three empty boxes, also. Under these conditions, 86 percent solved the problem. For the first group of people, the appearance of the boxes as containers for the supplies fixated them on the boxes-as-containers idea so much that they could not see beyond it (Mayer, 1992, pp. 57-59).

Functional fixity extends beyond things, as well. There is a functional fixity of people ("She's an administrative assistant; we can't promote her to VP of marketing"). And there is a functional fixity even of businesses. In fact, there is a saying in the corporate world that many organizations fail to prosper because when change comes, they do not know what business they are in. The following example clarifies this:

Example 2.3.2.2

In the nineteenth century, the railroads grew rapidly through passenger and freight hauling. In the twentieth century, airplanes began to carry people and freight as well, but the railroads just looked on. "We're in the railroad business, not the aviation business," they said. But if they had seen themselves as in the business of transporting people and freight rather than only in the railroad business, they could have taken advantage of a great opportunity to expand and modernize by adding airplanes.

2.3.3 INSTANT JUDGMENT.

A bias toward criticism seems to be part of human nature, which may explain why instantly condemning every new idea is common behavior. Some people have even collected lists of reasons why a new idea should be immediately rejected. Do you recognize any familiar comments here?

- ◆ That will never work.
- ◆ That has never been tried before.
- ◆ That has already been tried.
- ◆ We've never done it that way.
- ◆ The current system works fine.
- ◆ No one else is doing it that way.
- ◆ That's not really necessary.
- ◆ That's silly (stupid, childish, foolish).
- ◆ That's not practical.
- ◆ That would be too much trouble.

The automatic "No!" can prove quite inhibiting to creative problem solving. Yet, criticizing an idea is often seen as a sign of greater insight because it implies that the criticizer has seen a fault that the proposer of the idea has not. There is indeed substantial room for analyzing and criticizing ideas during the creative process. The time, though, should be after the ideas have had the opportunity to be developed. See Section 2.5.3 below for a discussion about the desirability of suspending judgment.

2.3.4 PSYCHOLOGICAL BLOCKS.

Some creative ideas are avoided or rejected simply because we react unpleasantly to them or feel embarrassed by them. We always want our solutions to be elegant, clean, and neat. However, embarrassing solutions themselves may be ideal if they solve a problem well.

Example 2.3.4.1

Navy commandos in Vietnam overcame their blocks and put on women's pantyhose when they marched through the swamps and the jungle. The pantyhose cut down on the friction and rubbing from the plants and aided the men in removing the leeches after a mission.

Perhaps more important, what at first seem to be unpleasant ideas may lead to better solutions—refined analogues of the original. Almost any idea can become a stepping-stone for a better idea. (See Chapter 6, Section 6.4.3, for a discussion about stepping stones.)

Example 2.3.4.2

Medical doctors visiting a tribal village noted that when someone sustained a cut, tribesmen held giant ants against the wound. When the ant closed its pincers across the wound, the tribesmen twisted the ant's body off, leaving the head and closed pincers to act as a suture. The doctors imitated this pincer-closing technique by inventing the surgical staple.

Psychological blocks should not prevent us from solving a problem just because the solution seems odd or embarrassing.

2.4 ATTITUDES THAT STRENGTHEN CREATIVITY.

Both the potential for and practice of creativity can be increased in those who adopt the attitudes that facilitate the process. As with any other skill, a positive attitude will help enhance performance.

2.4.1 CURIOSITY.

Creative people want to know things—all kinds of things—just to know them. Knowledge does not require a reason. The question, "Why do you want to know that?" seems strange to the creative person, who is likely to respond, "Because I don't know the answer." Knowledge is enjoyable and often useful in strange and unexpected ways.

Next, knowledge, and especially wide-ranging knowledge, is necessary for creativity to flourish to its fullest. Much creativity arises from variations of something known or combinations of two things. Creative solutions are often suggested by analogy, comparing a similar thing or situation. The best ideas flow from a well-equipped mind. Nothing can come from nothing. Knowledge, in fact, strengthens our ability to understand the world, and makes learning easier. An important Key of Wisdom reminds us of this:

⚿— The more you know, the better you can see.

In addition to knowing, creative people want to know why. What are the reasons behind decisions, problems, solutions, events, facts, and so forth? Why this way and not another? And why not try this or that?

The curious person's questioning attitude toward life is a positive one, not a destructive one reflecting skepticism or negativism. (It may seem threatening because too often there is no good reason behind many of the things that are taken for granted.) To stimulate your curiosity, try the following:

- **Ask questions of everyone.** When you meet someone who works in an area you know nothing about, ask about it.
- **Ask the same question of different people.** When you compare the answers, you may be surprised to see how much they vary.
- **Ask questions even when you already know the answer.** You may discover another answer or a new approach.

2.4.2 CONSTRUCTIVE DISCONTENT.

In a sentence, constructive discontent reflects the attitude, "This is good, but I wonder how it can be improved." Thus, it is not a whining, griping kind of discontent, but the ability to see a need for improvement and to propose a method of making that improvement. Constructive discontent is a positive, enthusiastic discontent that avoids the thinking, "That's good enough."

Constructive discontent is necessary for a creative problem solver, for if you are happy with everything the way it is, you will not want to change anything. Only when you become discontent with something, when you see a problem, will you want to solve the problem and improve the situation. That is why constructive discontent has been called "a primary quality of the creative problem-solver" (Koberg & Bagnall, 1981, p. 12).

Another aspect of constructive discontent is the enjoyment of challenge. Creative people are eager to test their own limits and the limits of problems, willing to work hard, to persevere and not give up easily. Sometimes the discontent is almost artificial—they are not really unhappy with the current solution or situation, but they want to find something better just for the challenge of it and the opportunity to improve their own lives and those of others.

2.4.3 OPTIMISM.

By faith at first, and by experience later on, the creative thinker believes that something can always be done to eliminate or help alleviate almost every problem. Problems are solved by a commitment of time and energy, and where this commitment is present, few things are impossible.

The belief in the solvability of problems is especially useful early on in attacking any problem, because many problems at first seem utterly impossible and scare off the more faint-hearted. Those who take on the problem with confidence will be the ones most likely to think through or around the apparent impossibility of the problem.

2.4.4 SEEING THE GOOD IN THE BAD.

Creative thinkers, when faced with unfinished ideas or even poor solutions, do not reject them completely and turn to something else. Instead, they ask, "What's good about this?" because there may be something useful, even in the worst ideas.

Example 2.4.4.1

How can students be encouraged to improve their writing? Proposed solution: Spank their bottoms with a hickory stick. This is not a good solution, partly because it is probably illegal. But instead of rejecting it completely, why not ask, "What's good about this?" The proposed solution has the following advantages:

- It gives individual attention to the poor performers.
- It gives them public attention.
- It motivates other students, as well as the student being spanked.
- It is easy and costs nothing.

These advantages lead us to ask the next question: Can we adapt or incorporate some of these good things into a more acceptable solution, whether derivative of the original or not? (One idea: Give public, hand-clapping applause to praise students who improve.)

2.4.5 BELIEVING THAT MISTAKES ARE WELCOME.

Making a mistake is often seen as something to be avoided at all costs. However, all risk is accompanied by a certain amount of failure and false starts, and risk taking is necessary whenever a solution is not obvious. Mistakes provide an opportunity to learn, and they show that something is being done. Therefore, creative thinkers realize and accept emotionally that making mistakes is an expected part of the problem-solving process. Mistakes are educational and can lead to success, as we are reminded by the following Key of Wisdom:

⚷— **It would not be called "trial and error" if every attempt worked.**

Example 2.4.5.1

Sir Francis Pettit Smith, one of the early developers of the screw propeller, tried a design in 1836. During the test, half the propeller broke off. Before Smith even had time to think, "That was a mistake," the boat increased in speed substantially, revealing the efficiency of a new design. His failure was a complete success.

2.4.6 PROBLEMS LEAD TO IMPROVEMENTS.

In the absence of an obvious problem, we often get stuck in the rut of complacency and endure whatever the current situation involves. The expression, "If it ain't broke, don't fix it," reveals this attitude. For this reason, sometimes an unexpected and unwanted problem can actually be an opportunity to make things better than ever before.

Example 2.4.6.1

The first margarine was made from beef fat, milk, water, and chopped cow udder. It was neither very tasty nor healthy, but it was in high demand because it was an inexpensive butter substitute. Then, near the beginning of the twentieth century, a shortage of beef fat created a problem. What could be done? The margarine makers turned to vegetable fats from various plants; and the soybean, corn, and sunflower oils they began using then are still used today. The margarine became healthier and better tasting.

It follows, then, that creative thinkers view problems as opportunities to create a better future, as stimuli for improving the current world, rather than as odious things to be fled from or denied. In fact, many creative thinkers are problem seekers, always on the lookout for a new problem to tackle.

2.4.7 A PROBLEM CAN ALSO BE A SOLUTION.

If you have ever driven along country roads, you may have seen an antique store with the sign, "We buy junk and sell antiques." The idea that one person's trash is another person's treasure applies to problems as well. Occasionally, what is a problem seen from one perspective may be a solution or benefit when seen from another angle.

Example 2.4.7.1

Chemists at the 3M company were experimenting with adhesives and accidentally came up with one that was so weak it would not hold on: Whatever was glued on with it could be peeled right back off. A glue that cannot hold? Quite a problem. But this problem became a solution, as you now see in Post-It® notes.

2.5 BEHAVIORS THAT STRENGTHEN CREATIVITY.

The most successful problem solvers exhibit several behaviors that improve their effectiveness as creative thinkers.

2.5.1 PERSEVERANCE.

Creativity and problem solving are hard work and require fierce application of time and energy. There is no quick and easy secret. Knowledge gained by study and research must be combined with hard thinking, new ideas, and protracted experimentation. The ability to stick to a task, to approach a problem from many angles, to continue striving after each dead end—this is the key to success. Planning to persevere is planning to succeed.

2.5.2 CHALLENGING THE *STATUS QUO*.

Curious people like to identify and challenge the assumptions behind problems (the current situation) and ideas (the proposed solutions). Many assumptions, of course, turn out to be quite necessary and solid, but many others have been assumed unnecessarily, and in breaking out of those assumptions often comes a new idea. When someone says, "That's the way it is," the creative thinker wants to know why. Does it have to be that way? Is there a better way?

Example 2.5.2.1

For hundreds of years, a college was automatically thought of as a physical campus with classrooms, a library, and some nice trees. Then someone asked, "But why must college be a *place* at all?" Thus, today many students "go to college" by staying at home and enrolling in distance-learning programs.

See Chapter 4, Section 4.2, for a discussion of assumption articulation during the problem-solving process.

2.5.3 THE ABILITY TO SUSPEND JUDGMENT AND CRITICISM.

As mentioned in Section 2.3.3 above, new ideas often receive a negative response simply because they are new. The unfamiliarity of the new makes many of these ideas seem strange, odd, bizarre, even repulsive. Only later do they become universally praised. Other ideas, in their original incarnations, are indeed weird, but they can lead to ideas that are practical and even beautiful. Therefore, it is important for the creative thinker to be able to suspend judgment when new ideas are arriving, to have an optimistic attitude toward ideas in general, and to avoid condemning them out of hand. Creative thinkers like to work with new ideas by asking questions like these:

- ◆ Can you tell me more about this?
- ◆ How can this be made to work?
- ◆ What else does this suggest?
- ◆ What do you like about this idea?
- ◆ What is good about this?

Example 2.5.3.1

Some of our everyday tools that we now love and use daily were opposed when they were originally presented: Aluminum cookware? No one wants that. Teflon pans? They'll never sell. Erasers on pencils? That would only encourage carelessness. Computers? There's no market for more than a few, so why build them? Hospital sterilization and antiseptic procedures, television, radio, the Xerox® machine, all met with ho-hums and even hostile rejection before their persevering inventors finally sold someone on their value.

Remember, then, that (1) an idea may begin to look good only after it becomes a bit more familiar or is seen in a slightly different way, and (2) even a very wild idea can serve as a stepping-stone to a practical, efficient idea. By too quickly bringing judgment into play, these fragile early ideas can be destroyed, leaving the world without the wonderful solutions they might have produced.

2.5.4 MENTAL PLAYFULNESS.

Creative people are comfortable with imagination and with thinking wild thoughts, not just for the sake of stimulation, but because those thoughts often lead in productive directions. While working out a problem, a creative thinker may mentally transform a French fry into a wall, then into a bench, and then into a road. Questions such as, "I wonder what that ball bearing feels like when it runs out of grease?" or "I wonder what the effect of squirt guns would be on parent-child counseling?" might occur in the normal course of flexible thinking.

Creative thinkers are always imagining the world as it is not. They ask, "What if?" of the world. (See Appendix A, Activity A.5.) The importance and power of asking "What if?" to look at a possible new reality is reinforced by the following Key of Wisdom:

⚷ Everything made by human hands had first to be imagined by human minds.

A final aspect of mental playfulness is that creativity, play, and humor are all connected. It is no coincidence that some of the most striking occurrences of sustained creativity are contained in classic cartoons such as those involving

Sylvester and Tweety, the Roadrunner, and the work of Tex Avery. Humor is an excellent stimulus for creative thinking because it encourages the mental playfulness needed for creating and connecting widely different ideas.

Characteristics of Creative People	
Curiosity	Why? How does this work?
Flexibility	How else? What other?
Openness to change	Let's try it. How can we improve this?
Imagination	How might we make this work? What if this were the case?
Independence	I don't care if no one else likes this.
Risk Taking	I'm not afraid to fail. Let's take a chance.
Optimism	Don't worry; we'll figure this out.
Perseverance	Let's try again. I'm not giving up.

QUESTIONS FOR REVIEW AND DISCUSSION.

1. Instead of viewing problems as something unpleasant to be avoided, how might you view problems in positive ways?

2. Define *learned helplessness* and explain how it might be overcome.

3. Why is it useful to solve a problem that already has a solution in place?

4. Discuss how someone might overcome *functional fixity*.

5. What is meant by a "bias toward criticism," and what effect does it have on creative problem solving? How can it be remedied?

6. Explain the benefits that problem solvers receive from asking questions.

7. Distinguish between *constructive discontent* and mere complaining.

8. If a creative problem solver sees a glass with water halfway up to the top, would he or she see the glass as half full or half empty? Support your conclusion with several examples. (See Sections 2.4.3 through 2.4.7 for ideas, if necessary.)

9. Why is it crucial for creative problem solvers to be able to suspend judgment and criticism when exploring ideas?

Chapter 3

❖

Identifying Problems

In order to solve a problem, you first have to know what the
problem really is, in the same way that you can't untie a knot
until you've found the knot.
—Aristotle

The best way to escape from a problem is to solve it.
—Brendan Francis

If you drive down the street and see a house on fire, identifying the immediate problem is fairly straightforward. However, many problems are either collections of several subproblems or are themselves the effects of underlying problems. What at first appears to be the problem may be only a symptom of an underlying problem. Similarly, identifying the cause of a problem often requires some extended investigation and thought. This chapter helps clarify the nature of problems by covering the following points:

- A problem exists when someone identifies a desired change in a situation.
- Hurrying to solve an unwelcome problem may result in failure to solve it well.
- Many problems are the result of one or more previous causes, and understanding the nature of causation is necessary for good solutions.

3.1 WHAT IS A PROBLEM?

Before we can answer even the most fundamental question of problem solving, "Does a problem exist?" we need to understand what a problem is. Understanding how problems are defined will help reduce confusion about their identification.

3.1.1 TYPES OF PROBLEMS.

The word *problem* covers a range of circumstances. A rapidly spreading computer virus is obviously an undesirable situation or problem in need of remedy, but the desire to improve a wristwatch design that already works well can also be called a problem, though in the sense of being a chosen challenge. The virus problem has a cause outside the solver, while the watch problem is one created by the solver.

Problems, then, fall into two broad types.

- **Externally caused.** This type of problem occurs when something fails or goes wrong and is the source of the negative sense of the word. A forest fire, a dam breaking, an illness, and a bankruptcy are all examples. In each case, the problems have discoverable causes.
- **Deliberately chosen.** This type of problem is one created by the solver and consists of a challenge or goal established in order to invent, improve, or remedy something. Improving the telephone, inventing a new way to hold shoes on feet, and designing a more comfortable office space are all examples.

3.1.2 DEFINITION.

An inclusive definition of *problem* must be broad enough to include both kinds mentioned above. In Chapter 2, Section 2.1.1, several suggested definitions of a problem were provided, most of them sharing the idea that a problem is the difference between a current situation and an ideal situation. Expressing this idea in a somewhat more general way, we arrive at our working definition of a problem.

> A **problem** is a situation someone wants to change.

The reason for this level of generality is that a given situation may not be viewed as a problem by everyone. A problem is a problem only when someone defines it as such.

Example 3.1.2.1

John decides to have some leftover pizza for lunch, so he takes it out of the refrigerator. The oven is broken. Is there a problem? If John likes his pizza hot, he has a problem. If he prefers it cold, he does not have a problem.

This example is admittedly simplistic, but it does reveal that in many cases the existence of a problem is a matter of definition or attitude. (Another example is that of improving the wristwatch, mentioned above.) As a result, it is important to identify the situation *as a problem* as clearly as possible. Whether you must explain a problem to someone else or whether the problem is being assigned to you by someone else, these questions should be answered along the way:

- What is the problem?
- Why is this a problem?
- What would you like to have instead?

Chapter 4 provides further information about describing and clarifying problems as an aid in understanding them and approaching solutions.

3.1.3 SUBPROBLEMS.

A subproblem is a smaller problem that is part of the larger one. Breaking the main problem down into subproblems is often the best way to solve it, especially if the main problem is large (such as water pollution, rural poverty, or the need to reduce electrical consumption in a factory). Even relatively small problems that may have multiple causes can benefit from a breakdown into subproblems. See Example 3.3.5.1 (page 33) relating to the causes of poor gasoline mileage in a car.

3.1.4 THE IMPORTANCE OF GOALS.

As mentioned above, several definitions of a problem were offered in Chapter 2, Section 2.1.1. One of those is, "A problem is an insight into the difference between what you have and what you want." Knowing what you want, then, is essential for knowing exactly what and how severe the problem is. In problem-solving terms, "what you want" is called the *goal state*. Not having clear goals can leave the problem ill-defined.

Example 3.1.4.1

The board of directors looked over a report from one of its divisions and noted that the text was vague, poorly written, and filled with typographical errors. The board therefore sent the report to an administrative assistant with the note, "Needs to be improved." The assistant added a few pictures and sent it back.

The word *improved*, of course, provides an unclear goal even though it sounds like an appropriate one. The assistant's lack of understanding of the problem came directly from the poor statement of goals.

More information about the nature and importance of goals will be found in Chapter 5.

3.1.5 OWNERSHIP.

Because problem solving can be a difficult and messy process ending in a solution that may be a challenge to implement (because of the resistance to change that meets many new ideas), the problem-solving process must be owned by those affected. If a group of people is involved, there must be agreement about the nature of the problem as well as a commitment to solve it. Groups working together on a problem not only pool their creativity and experience, but also apply their varied perspectives to create a consensus view of the definition of the problem.

3.2 INHIBITORS TO EFFECTIVE PROBLEM SOLVING.

The unpleasantness usually associated with problems (or even with the idea of having a problem) and the frequent haste people feel to get rid of problems combine to diminish the most effective solving process.

3.2.1 HOT-POTATO PROBLEM SOLVING.

Just as players in a game of hot potato toss the potato from one person to another as quickly as possible to avoid being burned, those who adopt this strategy really do not solve any problems: They merely pass them on to others, either by disclaiming responsibility ("That's the accounting department's issue, not ours") or by engaging in blame transfer ("That's not a hardware problem; it's a software problem").

3.2.2 PREMATURE CLOSURE.

The desire to get rid of a problem as quickly as possible can result in adopting the first course of action that appears at all likely to solve the problem. Leaping onto the first solution that comes to mind, however, can be costly and ineffective. As you will see in the next chapter, many expert problem solvers view problem exploration as the most important step in the problem-solving process.

3.2.3 DENIAL.

Denial may take the form of claiming that a problem does not exist at all, or it may involve claiming that what obviously appears to be the problem really is not, but that some other, more socially or personally acceptable thing is the real problem. In either case, the actual problem usually continues to get worse until it forces those involved to admit its existence.

> **Example 3.2.3.1**
>
> A family awoke one morning to discover that their sofa was broken in half. "Our problem is that we need a stronger sofa," they said. The next morning, the family noticed that many of their pictures were smashed and trampled into the floor. "The problem is that we put the pictures on the table instead of high up on the wall," they said. Two days later, the family came home to discover the television set had been kicked in. "We can solve this by putting the set in the bedroom," they said. Finally, one of the neighbors spoke up. "You know, maybe you should do something about the elephant in your living room."

Symbolic stories about "the elephant in the living room" are often used to teach about denial and the addressing of external effects rather than personal problems such as alcoholism or drug abuse. But these stories also remind us that denial can cause the misdirection of attention in any problem situation.

3.2.4 SOLVING THE WRONG PROBLEM.

Failure to take sufficient time to identify and explore a problem will often result in solving the wrong problem. Treating a symptom of a problem rather than the problem itself, attacking what appears to be the problem but what is really not a problem at all, and removing only part of the cause of a problem are all examples of solving the wrong problem. One of the behaviors that distinguishes expert from beginning problem solvers is that experts take much more time to identify and understand the problem itself before they begin to consider possible solutions. Beginners tend to jump toward a solution right away, even while the problem is ill-understood.

3.3 CAUSATION.

An important step in identifying a problem to be addressed is the analysis of causation. Through a careful study of cause and effect, we can trace problems (often appearing as effects) back to one or more causes that can be addressed. Consider these problem statements:

- ◆ Revenues are down.
- ◆ The television set does not work.
- ◆ Jane feels ill.
- ◆ Employees are coming in late.
- ◆ Graffiti is increasing in the south side.

All these immediately cause us to ask, "Why?" which is another way of asking, "What is the cause of these effects?"

3.3.1 WHAT IS A CAUSE?

When you accidentally kick a piece of furniture with your bare foot, you immediately know the cause of your pain. Clearly, the cause is your kicking the furniture. Causation, though, can quickly become more complex than this simple illustration. For example, going barefoot rather than wearing shoes must be in part responsible for your pain, so that also must be at least a partial cause. If you had not been walking, you would not have kicked the furniture, so your walking is also a partial cause of your pain.

Before we continue, we will adopt a working definition.

> A **cause** is an event, circumstance, or condition involved in producing an effect.

The words *event, circumstance,* and *condition* could be expanded to include *person, state of affairs, substance,* and many other terms, but you can see that we are speaking here of agency—the what or who contributing to the effect. The second part of the definition is the more important, however. By *involved* we mean that a circumstance or agent had *some role* in producing the effect, even though that role may have been minor. Causation, then, can exist in degrees. This idea brings us to the next section, about kinds of causes.

3.3.2 KINDS OF CAUSES.

In the previous section, we used the expression *partial cause* to indicate that a circumstance was not enough by itself to produce the effect (the pain in your foot). A more formal term for partial cause is *contributory cause*. Here is an explanation of the various kinds of causes that can act to produce an effect.

- ♦ **Sufficient cause.** A sufficient cause is an agent that by itself can produce a given effect. For example, spraying an insect with insecticide is a sufficient cause of its death; running out of gas is sufficient cause for engine failure; poor credit is often a sufficient cause for being denied a loan.

- ♦ **Necessary cause.** A necessary cause is an agent that must be present for an effect to occur, but which by itself cannot produce the effect. For example, the presence of oxygen in the air is a necessary cause for a forest fire (but not a sufficient cause); leaving a paint can open where you are painting is a necessary but not sufficient cause of the can spilling on the carpet; never backing up your files is a necessary but not sufficient cause of losing data.

- ♦ **Contributory cause.** A contributory cause is an agent that helps to bring about a given effect but which by itself is neither sufficient nor necessary. For example, a pothole in the street may have contributed to the crash of an intoxicated driver (but was neither sufficient by itself nor necessary to bring about a crash); the glorification of violence by the entertainment industry is likely a contributory cause of violence in young children; the speed the *Titanic* was going was a contributory cause to its sinking.

- ♦ **Proximate cause.** The proximate cause is the agent or event occurring immediately before the effect. In many cases, however, the proximate cause is itself the effect of a previous cause. In such cases, eliminating the proximate cause will not solve the underlying problem. For example, nearby moisture can enable dry rot (a moisture-loving fungus) to spread in wood. Wiping up the moisture may not cure the problem unless the source of the moisture is attended to. (See Section 3.3.4 (pages 31-33) for further discussion.)

Clearly, then, a given effect (or problem, in our case) can be the result of several causes, each with a different role to play in bringing about the effect.

3.3.3 FALLACIES OF CAUSATION.

As you seek to identify a problem and its cause or causes, you should be aware of three associated fallacies.

- *Post hoc, ergo propter hoc.* The English for this Latin phrase is "after this; therefore, because of this." The fallacy, known as *post hoc* for short, occurs when someone assumes that simply because event A occurred before event B, then event A must have caused event B to happen. In other words, the thinker is mistaking a time sequence (A, then B) for a cause-and-effect relationship (A caused B). Such a conclusion is plausible because the process of cause and effect does require such a sequence in time. However, the mere presence of a sequence is not sufficient to establish cause and effect. For example, someone might argue that a new principal is incompetent because school test scores are down a year after the principal came. But the lower scores could have been caused by factors taking place before the principal came or existing outside the principal's control.

- *Cum hoc, ergo propter hoc.* The *cum hoc* fallacy ("with this; therefore, because of this") mistakes a correlation between two things with a cause-and-effect relationship. For example, an advertiser might imply that the winner of an auto race won because a particular brand of motor oil was used, when, in fact, the driver would probably have won the race by using any effective motor oil. *Distinguishing between mere correlation and true cause and effect is one of the greatest challenges of causation analysis.*

- **Causal reduction.** This fallacy occurs when a single agent is named as *the* cause of an effect that actually is the result of several causes. As you have seen above, there are several kinds of causes, and many effects are the result of a number of contributory causes. To identify only one of these and hail it as the lone cause is to commit this fallacy. For example, to argue that a burglary was caused by a broken security light would be to commit this fallacy because several other causes (perhaps the burglar's drug habit, lack of police patrol, temptation of the goods inside the building, etc.) would be involved as well.

3.3.4 CHAIN OF CAUSATION.

Many problems are merely the end product of a chain of causes and effects. One thing causes an effect, which then causes another effect, which causes another effect, and so on. This sequence of cause-and-effect events can be described and diagrammed as a chain of causation, as the example below shows.

Example 3.3.4.1

A company noticed that one leg of its photocopier had begun to penetrate the floor. An examination of the floor revealed that it had developed dry rot. Further investigation revealed that the floor in the water heater closet next to the copier was wet, the result of a leaking pipe connected to the water heater. A few months earlier, a ladder had been moved into the closet and had apparently bumped against the pipe hard enough to produce the leak.

The following diagram reveals the chain of causation as it has been established.

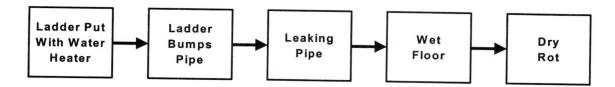

Chain of Causation for Dry Rot

As we walk down the chain of causation from the problem (the dry rot), we come to the proximate cause (the wet floor next door). Attacking this cause by mopping it up would help only briefly because it is itself the result of a previous cause, the leaking pipe. Fixing the leaking pipe is a much better place to *break the chain of causation* than mopping up the floor. Of course, the floor should also be mopped, and moving the ladder so that it cannot break the pipe again would also be a good idea.

In this example, laying out a chain of causation reveals several solutions or areas that should be addressed in order to remedy the problem permanently. Instead of merely fixing the floor (a symptomatic treatment), the underlying causes have been analyzed and can be addressed appropriately.

A caution should be observed in chain-of-causation analysis: Walking the chain beyond its reasonable breaking place(s) may lead to absurdity. Suppose we continue to walk the chain in the example above.

Example 3.3.4.1, continued

Further investigation revealed that the ladder was moved to the water heater closet because of inadequate storage space in the office suite. The inadequate storage space had been caused by the conversion of a storeroom into an office for a new employee who was hired when all the regular offices were already full. The new employee was needed because the business was growing rapidly.

Thus, to take the chain of causation to an absurd conclusion, it might be said that the rotting floor was caused by the rapid growth of the business. But to suggest solving the problem by reversing the growth of the business would be ridiculous.

Extended Chain of Causation for Dry Rot

3.3.5 MULTIPLE CAUSATION.

Even conceptually simple problems may turn out to be the result of many causes, so taking the time to perform an analysis of causation is beneficial for avoiding some of the inhibitors to problem solving discussed in Section 3.2 and for identifying the causes that can be most reasonably addressed.

Example 3.3.5.1

The rise in gasoline prices causes you to check the gas mileage on your car. To your dismay, the car is getting poor mileage. What could be the cause of this? There are several possible contributory causes, including the weight of the car, the condition of the engine, the tires, and even the air resistance of the car as it rolls down the road. Some of these possible causes have contributory causes of their own. For example, the vehicle's empty weight, the cargo in the trunk, and the number of passengers all contribute to the overall weight of the car.

As a way of understanding these causes and their relationship, a fishbone diagram can be created, as shown below.

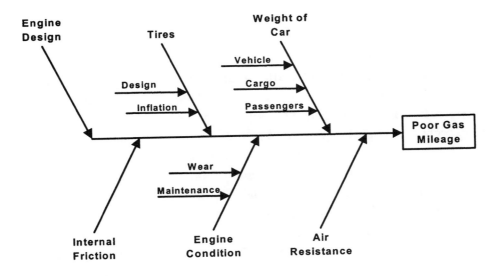

Fishbone Diagram of Multiple Causes

Note that one advantage to a thorough analysis drawn into a diagram like this is that each cause can be evaluated for its role in the effect (problem) and for the desirability or possibility of addressing it. In this diagram, for example, addressing the problem of the engine design would be unlikely (a new engine would need to be installed in order to change the design), while addressing the problem of tire inflation would be simple. Similarly, little can be done about the vehicle's empty weight, but the cargo in the trunk (a set of barbells, perhaps) can be reduced or removed.

Complex problems often have not only multiple contributory causes but multiple interacting causes, where a number of causative agents influence each other, as well as ultimately produce the final effect. The following example illustrates this:

Example 3.3.5.2

On January 25, 1990, Avianca Flight 52 crashed while attempting to land in New York. The proximate or immediate cause of the crash was the failure of all four engines, which in turn was caused by the aircraft running out of fuel.

It would be strange indeed if sophisticated aircraft simply ran out of fuel unpredictably. Thus, to conclude that the root or actionable cause of the crash was fuel exhaustion would almost certainly lead to a merely symptomatic treatment rather than to a solution that would prevent future similar occurrences. In this particular case, a continued analysis of the situation (including asking, "Why did the aircraft run out of fuel?") reveals a much more complex collection of factors.

Example 3.3.5.2, continued

An investigation by the National Transportation Safety Board revealed that bad weather and poor FAA traffic management combined to create holding patterns for landing aircraft at the airport. A lack of standardized fuel terms for revealing when fuel was *critically low* (as opposed to simply *low*), and the failure of the crew to use a dispatch system to assist them as they flew into the high traffic area of New York combined to create a communication failure that resulted in the aircraft being put into three holding patterns, totaling more than an hour, even though it was very low on fuel. Flying the three holding patterns not only used up most of the remaining fuel on board, but it added to the fatigue of the crew. That fatigue, added to wind shear near the airport (caused by the bad weather), caused the crew to miss the first approach to the airport. The aircraft ran out of fuel while flying back around for another approach. (National Transportation Safety Board, n.d.)

To understand better the interaction of causal factors in this case, we can construct a matrix of causation. If you read the arrows to mean *contributed to*, you will see how a confluence of many factors led to the final result.

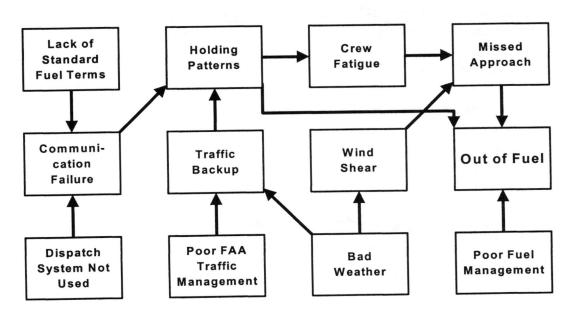

Matrix of Causation for Flight 52

Solving this problem, then, requires a number of changes in procedure, ranging from communications to traffic management to fuel management, and so on.

A useful tool for working with causation is the multidirectional why. See Chapter 6, Section 6.3.1.

QUESTIONS FOR REVIEW AND DISCUSSION.

1. Comment briefly on each of the following definitions of a problem. Which definition do you think is the best, and why?
   (a) A problem is something bad that needs to be fixed.
   (b) A problem occurs when someone identifies a deficiency.
   (c) A problem is created by the occurrence of a negative causal event.
   (d) A problem is the difference between an actual and a desired state.

2. What is the danger of walking a chain of causation too far?

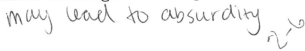

3. What is the risk of treating a proximate cause as the only cause of a problem? *B/c proximate causes often are the effect of previous causes*

4. Distinguish between a chain of causation and multiple causation.
Chain → cause & effect etc. many problems, multiple → one problem

5. Read the following account and construct a fishbone diagram reflecting the contributing causes. Below is a partial diagram with hints that you may use if you wish. You may also construct your own from scratch.

A homeowner cleaned a bicycle with a flammable solvent in the garage. The rags used were made of cotton cloth. The solvent-soaked rags were dumped in a pile near a gas-fired water heater. Lumber was also stored near the water heater. The day was hot. The garage was poorly ventilated. Fumes built up and were ignited by the water heater, causing a fire in the garage.

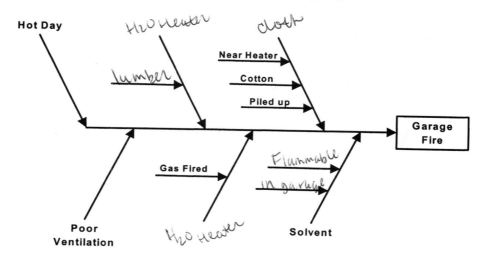

6. For each instance below, decide whether the event presented is most likely a sufficient cause, a necessary cause, or a contributory cause.
   (a) Watering a plant to make it grow. — N
   (b) Obtaining a credit card to establish a credit rating. — S
   (c) Draining a lake to kill an undesirable species of fish. — N S
   (d) A legal assistant's misunderstanding of an attorney's verbal instructions as a cause of an error in a contract. — C & S
   (e) Electrical service as a cause of a house fan running. — N
   (f) Long exposure to sunlight as a cause of paint fading. — C

Chapter 4

The Problem-Solving Cycle 1
Exploring the Problem

Great doubts bring great understanding; little doubts bring
little understanding.
—Chinese Proverb

The first to present his case seems right, till another comes for-
ward and questions him.
—Proverbs 18:17

Once a problem has been identified, it can be worked on through a six-step
problem-solving cycle. This chapter covers the first step in the cycle, Exploring
the Problem, and each chapter following covers a subsequent step.

> **The Problem-Solving Cycle**
> ➜ Exploring the Problem ⬅
> Establishing Goals
> Generating Ideas
> Choosing the Solution
> Implementing the Solution
> Evaluating the Solution

This chapter emphasizes the following aspects of problem exploration:
- The way a problem is defined has a significant bearing on how effectively it is eventually solved.
- The assumptions made about a problem situation can help focus the
  problem but can also block a solution.
- Approaching a problem from many angles allows a fuller understanding of the problem and of possible solution approaches.

4.1 DEFINE THE PROBLEM.

When you first ask, "What seems to be the problem?" you may be dealing
with a highly unstructured situation that requires some effort to understand.
Remember that you do not want to solve the wrong problem or a problem that
does not exist. Your goal at this point is to structure the problem so that it can
be understood and addressed. As you continue to work on the problem, the way
you describe and understand it will most likely change. However, expressing the

problem as clearly as possible at the outset will provide a useful beginning focus.

4.1.1 STATE THE PROBLEM.

Begin your exploration by writing down a statement of what the problem is in the way it has been presented to you. Then describe the problem in your own words. As you look at these statements, remember this Key of Wisdom:

The initial statement of a problem often reflects a preconceived solution.

As you continue to explore the problem, you may need to alter the statement to eliminate the preconceived solution.

Note that in each of the following example problem statements, a preconceived solution path is stated or implied.

- "Develop a more effective punishment that will reduce absenteeism." [Better: "Develop a means to reduce absenteeism."]
- "How can we move our offices to a quieter area?" [Better: "How can we produce a quieter work environment?"]

4.1.2 CLARIFY THE PROBLEM.

Complex problems seldom arrive with complete clarity, and, in fact, there is a danger in assuming that a problem is clearer than it actually is. Taking a closer look is always a good idea.

- **Investigate the problem area.** The same or similar problem may have been faced by others. If so, how did they solve it? Research can save enormous time and effort in problem solving because you may be able to use the same solution, adapt a previous solution, or at least gain some valuable ideas (starting points, knowledge about what will not work, stimuli for further thinking, and so on).
- **Define the terms.** A significant source of miscommunication is the use of the same word by two people who have different understandings of the word. Another source of miscommunication is the use of terms that have not been clearly defined. Defining the terms central to the problem will avoid both of these sources of miscommunication. For example, what is meant by *short battery life*? Does that refer to a battery that requires recharging in an hour or a battery that must be replaced after only six months?
- **Research the history of the problem itself.** When did the problem begin? Where did it come from? What are its causes? Why is it a problem? Who first defined it? (See Chapter 3, Section 3.3, for a discussion about causation.) Remember the "Journalistic Six" questions: Who? What? When? Where? How? Why?

- **Discuss the problem with someone else.** The mere act of verbalizing a problem can help clarify it for you, so even if you discuss the problem with someone who has little knowledge of the problem area, you can gain some valuable insights into your own thinking and possibly see the problem in a new way. Discussing the problem with a knowledgeable person may result in some good suggestions or approaches.

4.1.3 RESTATE THE PROBLEM.

Using the information and insights gained from clarifying the problem, together with your own creative thinking, restate the problem. Be careful not to limit the problem statement too narrowly. The formulation of a problem determines the range of choices, so if the description is too narrow, the range of choices will be unnecessarily limited. Compare the following questions and note the different ideas arising from questioning and restating the problem.

- Where can we get the money to build more classrooms for our increasing student population?
- How can we make better use of the classrooms that we have?
- What other ways than a traditional classroom might we bring students together for instruction?
- How can students be instructed without needing to be in a traditional classroom?

Just in these few restatements of the problem, the focus has ranged from fundraising to considerations that might involve teaching students in their homes or dormitory rooms by using the Internet. The restatement about better use of current classrooms might lead to a discussion of room management software, while the idea of a nontraditional classroom might lead to classes under the trees or in remote locations such as a museum. Remember that the questions you ask help determine the answers you receive. The following Key of Wisdom reminds us of this:

⚷ To get a better answer, ask a better question.

When you work on problem restatements, try to use entirely different words. Write at least three different statements; half a dozen may be even better. Statements that reflect different approaches to the problem are superior to statements that merely say the same thing using other words.

4.1.4 REPRESENT THE PROBLEM ABSTRACTLY.

Describing the problem as an abstract or philosophical issue will often broaden the approach to it and supply some new creative ways to solve it. One of the most powerful strategies for problem solving is reconceptualization:

thinking about the problem in a new way. (See Chapter 1, Sections 1.2.2 and 1.3.4 for more information.) The problem can be gradually broadened, thought of in ever more general terms, or it can be taken immediately to a highly abstract state and then gradually made more concrete and specific.

Example 4.1.4.1

Initial problem: How to move filing cabinets closer to our offices to make research more convenient. Abstract conceptualization: This is a problem of information access. Can a system be devised where the information can be brought to the worker's desk from its storage location? (In former times, this might have suggested pneumatic tubes carrying folded paper; today it might suggest digitizing the files and making the information available on a computer.)

Example 4.1.4.2

Initial problem: Improve a mattress to aid sleepers with bad backs. Abstract conceptualization: This is a problem of how to sleep. Do we need a better mattress, a better bed, or a new way to sleep? Is a design like that of a recliner chair more suitable for this than a new mattress?

Experienced problem solvers think of their problems in abstract terms because this activity provides several benefits.

- **New approaches.** Abstraction makes it easier to approach the problem in a new way.
- **More solutions.** Abstraction allows for the creation of many more ideas for possible solutions.
- **Context.** Abstraction places the problem in a wider context, helpful for understanding the relation of the problem to the rest of the world.

A useful technique for abstracting is to move the problem concept from a thing to an action, as seen in the following examples:

Example 4.1.4.3

Design a better knife? That's really a problem about designing a better way to cut something.

Example 4.1.4.4

Improve our satisfaction ratings from visitors to the museum? That's really a problem about improving how visitors experience the museum.

4.2 ARTICULATE THE ASSUMPTIONS.

Assumptions shape the way a problem is approached and the possible solutions considered to solve it. The chief danger of assumptions lies in their often silent presence: They remain hidden and unrecognized until a deliberate effort is made to state them. Assumption articulation is the process of identifying and stating the assumptions surrounding a problem.

4.2.1 ASSUMPTIONS ARE NECESSARY.

Assumptions are shortcuts that enable us to make decisions and solve problems more efficiently. As such, many of them provide necessary benefits.

- **Assumptions set limits.** Time, money, effort and other resources are limited. Reasonable constraints circumscribe every problem because no person or organization has unlimited time, money, personnel, or technology.

- **Assumptions reflect desired values.** For example, when thinking about more effective punishments as deterrents for crime, we assume that the punishments will remain humane.

- **Assumptions help simplify the problem.** Assuming certain boundaries and methods of proceeding makes the problem more manageable because there are fewer variables to consider.

4.2.2 ASSUMPTIONS ARE OFTEN SELF-IMPOSED.

While many assumptions are necessary for making a problem understandable and manageable, many other assumptions are arbitrary and produce unnecessary constraints. When the problem solver is unaware of these self-imposed limits, they can inhibit or even prevent finding a solution. See the box below, "Customer States Car Will Not Start," for a real-life example and the care taken by professionals to avoid unnecessary assumptions.

Customer States Car Will Not Start

A motorist stopped for gasoline in his one-year-old car. When he turned the key after refueling, instead of the engine starting, the rear window wiper began to operate. A second turn of the key caused the front windshield wiper to operate but still not the engine. The car was towed to the dealer. "The car's computer must have gotten fried," the motorist told the service writer, "because instead of starting the car, it turned on the wipers."

The service writer carefully wrote on the service order, "Customer states car will not start."

Notice that in order not to prejudice their technicians, service writers do not write down any possible diagnosis, but give only the reported symptom. Even the symptom is qualified by "Customer states," meaning that the symptom itself is not even a guaranteed fact, only that the customer reports it.

The problem turned out to be a failed battery. The motorist had been trapped by an assumption—that the battery would not have failed after just a year. (The service writer explained that when the voltage in the battery drops to a very low level, the car's computer loses its mind and turns functions on randomly. However, when voltage is restored to normal levels, the computer is fine once again.)

An important part of problem exploration, then, is to question the assumptions created during assumption articulation.

- **Is the assumption correct?** If not, it should not be used to control the direction of the problem-solving process.
- **Is the assumption necessary?** If not, should it be eliminated?
- **If the assumption is not necessary, is it appropriate?** Assumptions that represent adopted constraints, such as the time allowed to complete a project or the maximum cost, may be arbitrary but still highly desirable.

Example 4.2.2.1

I put this tape in the VCR, and the tape will not play. Therefore, the tape is bad. What assumption am I making? I am assuming that the tape will not work in *any* VCR. Is that correct? Or should I conclude only that the tape will not work in *this* VCR and do another test before I throw the tape away? (And unless I know that this VCR will play other tapes, I might need to check that assumption, too.)

4.2.3 EXAMINE THE ASSUMPTIONS.

Make a list of the assumptions surrounding the problem. This list might be divided into three parts.

- **General assumptions.** These are the "obvious" assumptions made without thinking and often without realizing they have been made. Many of them are necessary, but some may not be. All deserve examination. For example, for this new product, we assume that we will use our usual suppliers. Or, we assume we will sell this product, not give it away.
- **Assumptions determining constraints.** These are the assumptions relating to cost, time, effort, government regulations, policies, and so forth that limit the solution. Once again, many of these are desirable or necessary, but sometimes they do not apply or can be modified.
- **Assumptions at the crux.** These are the assumptions right at the sticking point of the problem. They are usually made consciously, but they are often the source of the block to a solution. Examining them with special care will often result in a change of direction, the reconceptualization that is needed to solve the problem.

Example 4.2.3.1

Problem: The more often people visit a store and the longer they stay, the more they buy. But we are a department store that people usually visit only monthly or less. How can we get customers to visit more frequently? More ads? More sales? Assumption at the crux: People simply do not need our goods very often. Breaking the assumption: Why don't we add groceries? People need to visit the grocery store weekly, so if they came here for groceries, they would visit once a week—and might shop the rest of the store as well.

4.3 USE A 360-DEGREE APPROACH.

Essential to the best problem solving is the ability to perform a mental reaching around the problem to grasp it with the whole mind. To use another metaphor, if you imagine a problem as a three-dimensional object, the best understanding will come from looking at it from many different angles: top, bottom, and sides.

4.3.1 USE MULTIPLE VIEWPOINTS.

An excellent way to approach a problem from another direction is to get outside your own head and see the problem from the perspective of people different from you. Discussing the problem with others, as recommended in Section 4.1.2 (page 38) is one way to do this, of course. Another way is to imagine that you are some of the others involved with the problem.

Example 4.3.1.1

Problem: Reduce the litter on beaches. Viewpoints: What do the people doing the littering think about the situation? Are they thinking, "I enjoy littering"? Or are they thinking, "I would put this in a trashcan, but there isn't one nearby, so I'll just toss it on the ground"? Or might they think, "I see that trashcan over there, but it probably smells and I don't want to go near it"? What is the viewpoint of the person who picks up the trash? What do the other beachgoers think of trash on the beach or of trashcans? What is the perspective of those who do put the trash in the cans?

Example 4.3.1.2

Problem: Improve the juvenile justice system. Imagine that you are, in turn, the juvenile offender, the parents, the victim, a law enforcement officer, a judge, an ordinary citizen, and so on. By constructing these imaginary viewpoints (or by collecting real viewpoints through interviews), you might be able to see the problem in a more comprehensive and well-rounded way.

4.3.2 CREATE ALTERNATIVE EXPLANATIONS.

Chapter 1, Section 1.2.1 noted that defining and structuring a problem often requires creating a story from the available information. When the problem is highly unstructured, more than one story or explanation is often possible for the same information. Creating several alternative explanations increases the probability that the problem will be understood accurately, that one of the proposed explanations (known as hypotheses) will be correct. On the other hand, there are two dangers when only a single explanation is considered.

- **Some information will be missed or ignored.** Information that is relevant or even crucial to the problem, but that has no bearing on the one explanation being proposed, will be wrongly considered irrelevant to the problem.
- **Information that conflicts with the explanation will be discounted.** Allowing only a single explanation for a set of information often results in the unconscious use of a knowledge filter: Only evidence that supports the explanation is collected, while evidence that conflicts with it is denied or explained away.

When multiple possible explanations are on the table, all information can be accepted and put into one or another of them.

Example 4.3.2.1

At lunchtime Jane ate some bad-tasting food at a questionable diner. Around bedtime she began to feel ill. Her symptoms included nausea, stomach cramps, diarrhea, a runny nose, and a sore throat. There are two common possible explanations (diagnoses, in medical terms) for her symptoms, as seen by the diagram below. Note that neither explanation accounts for absolutely all the information (a common situation in problem solving), but that having two explanations allows the problem solver to focus on the information unique to each explanation.

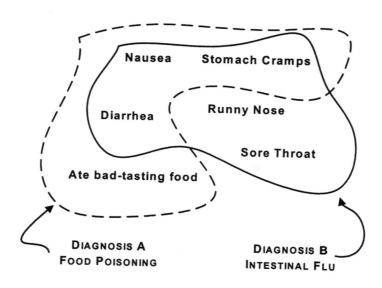

Alternative Explanations for the Available Information

4.3.3 SEEK DISCONFIRMING EVIDENCE.

When confronted by a mass of information, experienced problem solvers immediately begin to build multiple possible explanations (sometimes called rival hypotheses) and then seek evidence that supports each one. But they also take a further step: They seek evidence that argues *against* each hypothesis. They ask questions like the following:

- ◆ What evidence would make this explanation wrong or unlikely?
- ◆ Is there any of that evidence here?

Disconfirming evidence is important for testing one explanation against another, and the search for it often turns up more information useful in solving the problem. Information that argues against one explanation may then argue in favor of another. A robust search for disconfirming evidence for every hypothesis under consideration will also prevent the problem solver from becoming overly fond of any one explanation too early in the problem-solving process.

Comparison Between a Beginning and an Experienced Problem Solver	
As the following table reveals, the strategies recommended in this chapter reflect the characteristic behaviors of experienced problem solvers. The experienced problem solver takes a more active command of the problem than does the beginning problem solver.	
Beginning Problem Solver	**Experienced Problem Solver**
Works with the problem as stated.	Does not accept the original statement of the problem.
Represents the problem concretely.	Represents the problem in abstract terms.
Takes assumptions for granted.	Examines assumptions for necessity.
Develops a single explanation.	Develops multiple alternative explanations.
Reluctant to change to a new explanation.	Changes to new explanations easily.
Seeks only confirming evidence for the explanation.	Seeks both confirming and disconfirming evidence for all explanations.

(For more about the behavior of experienced problem solvers, see Mayer, 1992, Chapter 13, and Weisberg, 1993, pages 113-123.)

4.3.4 USE MULTIPLE POINTS OF ATTACK.

A point of attack is the aspect of the problem addressed first. Rather than always attacking a problem at some obvious point on the front end, consider some alternatives. Problems can be first attacked at any one of several front-end points, in the middle, and even at the end. (See de Bono, 1970/1973, Chapter 17, for more information.) The following example clarifies this.

Example 4.3.4.1

Problem: Make money from a commercial building rental.

Linear model:

Find Location—Hire Architect—Hire Contractor—Get Tenants

Front-end points of attack: Find a suitable lot; find a city with tax benefits; find a city with demand for office space.

Middle points of attack: Locate an architect; locate contractor who has the ability to complete the project.

End point of attack: Find tenants who need a new office building.

QUESTIONS FOR REVIEW AND DISCUSSION.

1. What is the preconceived solution embedded in each of these problem statements? What are some better ways to state the problem? +
   (a) How can we kill the rats in the warehouse on the dock? *How to are get rid of rats?*
   (b) How can we motivate students to take our voluntary assessment test on a Saturday?
   (c) How can we develop a stronger ignition key lock so that thieves cannot hotwire our cars so easily? *How do we prevent car theft*

2. What are the advantages of representing a problem abstractly in addition to its more concrete form? *Broaden approach to it & supply some new creative ways to solve it.*

3. Do assumptions help or hinder problem solving? Why or how? *Often remain hidden / unrecognized until deliberate effort is made to see them. Help & Hinder*

4. What is the role of disconfirming evidence in establishing a hypothesis or explanation? *Important for testing one explanation against another & usually turns up more useful info for solving it.*

5. The making of a Hollywood-style motion picture might be represented by the following linear model, where beginning with the idea would be a front-end point of attack. How might the order change if a middle point of attack were chosen? (Remember that "middle" can be anywhere between the ends.)

   Idea—Script—Producer—Studio—Actors—Filming—Advertising—Showing
   producer — studio — idea — script — actors — film — advertise — show

6. Suggest an alternative explanation (rival hypothesis) for each of the situations below.
   (a) Those who drink more than six cups of coffee a day have a higher rate of heart attacks than those who drink fewer cups. Hypothesis: Coffee causes heart attacks. *Those who drink coffee are more stressed, so that is cause of heart attack.*
   (b) An airliner crashed during a snowstorm in Colorado. Hypothesis: Zero visibility caused the pilot to become disoriented and lose control of the plane. *Ran out of fuel*
   (c) Several children in a junior high school report feeling ill in the afternoon. Hypothesis: A flu epidemic is beginning. *Food poisoning*

Chapter 5

❖

The Problem-Solving Cycle 2
Establishing Goals

In the beginning, look well and take good heed to the ending.
—*Everyman*

Who aimeth at the sky shoots higher much
than he that means a tree.
—George Herbert

Armed with a good, working understanding of the problem, you are ready to move to the next step of the problem-solving cycle, Establishing Goals.

> **The Problem-Solving Cycle**
> Exploring the Problem
> ➔ Establishing Goals ⬅
> Generating Ideas
> Choosing the Solution
> Implementing the Solution
> Evaluating the Solution

This chapter emphasizes the importance of goals:
- ◆ Goals are necessary for the appropriate selection of a solution.
- ◆ Values of many kinds influence the development of goals.
- ◆ Goals can be expressed in terms of criteria to be met.
- ◆ Ideal goals help improve the quality of finally selected practical goals.

5.1 THE NECESSITY OF GOALS.

In problem solving, goals are necessary to guide you toward the solution you should choose. A simple analogy is that of taking a vacation. You first determine where you want to go (the goal), and that decision guides you in the selection of the proper road or flight (the solution path) that takes you there. Talking about which road to take before you know where you want to go makes little sense. The same is true in problem solving. Before you begin to think about generating possible solutions to the problem you have explored, you should clarify the goals you want the solution to meet.

5.1.1 GOALS CLARIFY WHAT THE SOLUTION SHOULD LOOK LIKE.

Problems can be addressed by several kinds and degrees of solutions (see Chapter 7 for more discussion). The choice of solution depends on the goals. Do you want to eliminate the problem completely? Do you want to reduce the severity of the problem? Or will the solution be a means of adapting to the consequences of a problem that cannot be eliminated? Whatever the answer, for a given goal state, some solution paths may work while others will not. For a given goal state, the best solution path will likely be quite different from that needed for a different goal state. In other words, the desired goal state will determine the solution path. The illustration below clarifies this.

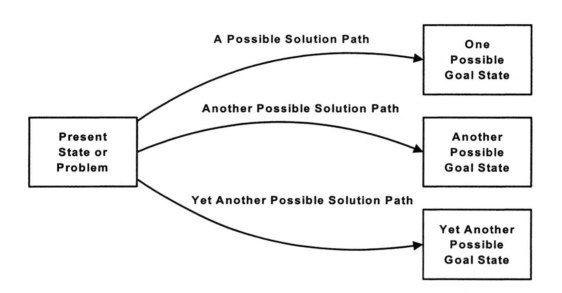

The Relationship Between a Goal State and a Solution Path

This diagram also reminds us of the importance of the effort spent on problem exploration in the last chapter. If our desire is to create a path (the solution) between the problem state and a specific goal state, we need to know clearly what the two states are. Only then can the solution path connect the two.

5.1.2 GOALS ESTABLISH A CONTEXT FOR THE REMAINING STEPS.

The structure of clearly knowing the problem and the goal provides guidance for the remaining steps in the problem-solving cycle. The goal informs the process of generating ideas (focused on the goal), choosing one or more of those ideas for the solution (using criteria developed from the goals), and evaluating the success of the solution (measuring the effect of the solution against the desired goals).

5.1.3 GOALS PROVIDE CRITERIA FOR SOLUTIONS.

When you generate ideas—whether two or twenty—that may solve the problem, you will need some way of evaluating them so that you can choose the best one. Goals provide the criteria (the standards or desirable qualities) for ranking and measuring the solution candidates. Goals, then, allow the problem solver to do the following.

- **Select the best solution from among the alternatives.** There may be several alternatives, each of which may solve the problem in a different way. Established goals will help in choosing the solution that works in the most desirable way.
- **Measure the success of the solution.** In the evaluation phase of problem solving, when we ask, "Did the solution work?" we need some reference points to use for answering the question. Goals serve as these reference points.
- **Keep the solution focused.** Often, solutions must be modified in the course of implementation. In such cases, clear goals keep the modifications consistent with each other and with the desires of the problem solver.

5.2 THE IMPORTANCE OF VALUES.

Goals are developed by reference to values. Values are the principles or beliefs about what is important (usually what is good or worthy) that guide us in our decision making. They allow us to rank, evaluate, and choose from among options.

5.2.1 KINDS OF VALUES.

In problem solving, we are surrounded by many sets of values, all of which may impact the goals we choose.

- **Corporate values.** Organizations hold many values relating to how they operate, how they relate to others, and the purposes of their existence. For example, customer satisfaction is a common corporate value.
- **Legal and regulatory values.** Societal values enacted into law result in regulations that must be observed. An example of this is the legal prohibition against dumping used motor oil into storm drains.
- **Ethical and religious values.** These values serve as a moral compass in problem solving. For example, a person or organization might consider it unethical to use sexual appeals in advertisements.

- **Personal values.** All of us have a set of personal values by which we make choices and rank alternatives. For example, when making or buying a certain product, one person might value usefulness above elegance of design, while another person might have the opposite value.

These values often overlap, as in a case where fairness might be a corporate, ethical, and personal value—and possibly even a legal one.

5.2.2 VALUES SIMPLIFY DECISION MAKING.

A solid set of values (written out in the case of an organization) simplifies the process of ranking alternatives and making decisions about solutions and goals because the criteria or standards for ranking already exist. Moreover, these values serve to focus the direction of the problem-solving activity.

Example 5.2.2.1

A dental HMO is concerned with efficiency, but its managers might adopt the value of enhancing the sense of personal care among its patients in order to increase customer satisfaction. Therefore, every new policy proposed to increase efficiency would always be tested by the question, "Will this enhance or reduce our patients' sense of personal care?"

As this example reveals, values can be thought of as a category of desired constraints that serve to limit the boundaries in the search for solutions.

5.2.3 VALUES ADD CONSISTENCY TO PROBLEM SOLVING.

Because values might be viewed as a set of standards or even rules of procedure, they add consistency to the problem-solving process by serving as operational guidelines. Similar to the function of a policy and procedure manual, values standardize the view of what is important. The hierarchy of importance remains constant across the process of problem solving (and for each problem), permitting a coherence to the decisions of the person or organization.

Without a defined set of values, problem solving is subject to three diminishments.

- **Drift.** Over time, the goals of the problem solvers change, perhaps without conscious awareness.
- **Expediency.** At a crux in the problem-solving process, which choice is to be made? Without guiding values, the tendency is always to take the easier of the two possibilities. Without clear values, there is a tendency to choose a quick fix or a shortcut to a solution. Billion-dollar recalls sometimes result.
- **Confusion.** Without guiding values, the establishment of goals may appear to be arbitrary, leading to confusion about how to proceed

with each new problem. Without a consistent set of values, solving one problem will not necessarily serve as a model for solving a new problem.

5.3 CONSIDER IDEAL GOALS.

As we have seen in Chapter 3, Section 3.2, a dislike of problems causes many people to look only at the immediate problem and to adopt the fastest solution to it. As a result, many of these solutions address only the symptoms of an underlying problem. Taking time to consider ideal goals, rather than remaining focused on an immediate quick fix, will improve the quality of the solution.

5.3.1 THINK BEYOND AN IMMEDIATE SOLUTION.

In the same way that experienced problem solvers go beyond the immediate definition of the problem and represent it in abstract terms (Chapter 4, Section 4.1.4), they also go beyond thinking about an immediate solution and consider an ideal one. Instead of asking, "What is the quickest or easiest way to remedy this?" they ask, "How would I like to see this situation ideally?"

> **Example 5.3.1.1**
>
> A husband and wife go to a marriage counselor. The wife complains that her husband disagrees with everything she says and criticizes everything she does. Her husband disagrees. The wife asks, "How can I get my husband to stop criticizing me so much?" The counselor knows that a more ideal goal would be for the husband not only to stop criticizing but to support and encourage his wife.

The diagram on the next page shows how an ideal goal can raise the bar for a practical goal. This diagram might be viewed as the visual version of the George Herbert quotation in the epigraph at the beginning of the chapter: If you aim high, you will shoot farther than if you aim low. When thinking about ideal goals, dream a little. Assume that nothing is impossible. Recall the caution of Chapter 4, Section 4.2: Do not be trapped by assumptions. Use creative thinking to envision a solution that goes beyond a merely adequate solution. Create an ideal future. And remember this Key of Wisdom (from Ackoff, 1978, p. 25):

🔑 **Our conception of possible outcomes affects what outcomes we desire.**

5.3.2 IDEAL GOALS ARE MOTIVATING.

An awareness of how reality would look if the problem solver's dreams came true not only can encourage the setting of higher practical goals but can motivate the solver to work harder toward them.

Example 5.3.2.1

Suppose a manufacturer's quality goals are to make its products 99 percent defect-free. This practical goal allows for one defect per 100 products, or 10,000 defects per million. Then suppose the manufacturer learns about a commonly used measure of quality known as Six Sigma. This quality goal allows a maximum of only 3.4 defects per million.

The resulting challenge of reducing defects per million from 10,000 to 3.4 should be highly motivating. While 99 percent once looked good, the knowledge that a much higher standard is possible produces the desire to strive harder toward it.

By thinking about ideal goals, you are not necessarily committing to bringing them about. Identifying ideal goals provides a reference point for developing the practical goals that will actually be pursued (see Section 5.4 below). The purpose of ideal goals is to help reduce the distance between the ideal and the real. You may never run the 100-meter dash in ten seconds, but seeing that time as an ideal should motivate you to strive for a better time than you otherwise might.

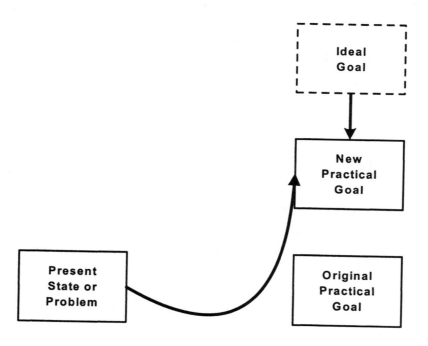

Ideal Goals Influence and Improve Practical Goals

5.4 ESTABLISH SPECIFIC, PRACTICAL GOALS.

The final task in the process of establishing goals is to construct the specific, practical goals the solution to the problem should meet. A good practice is to describe what the solved problem will look like. For example, the problem solver might write out a statement such as, "The problem will be solved when the following goals are met," followed by a specific list of factors. Realizing each of these factors becomes a separate practical goal.

5.4.1 SPECIFIC GOALS PROVIDE SPECIFIC TARGETS.

As mentioned in Chapter 3, Section 3.1.4, unclear goals can leave the problem itself poorly defined and thus difficult to attack. Specific goals, by contrasting with the problem state, help clarify the problem itself. By providing a definite target, specific goals provide other benefits as well.

◆ **Specific targets provide a completion test.** Unclear goals prevent the problem solver from knowing when the problem has been solved. For example, if the stated goal is to "reduce unemployment," how will the problem solver know when the goal is met? On the other hand, the goal to "reduce unemployment for both males and females over age eighteen to five percent within the next two years" gives the problem solver an exact, measurable target against which the results of the solution can be measured.

◆ **Specific targets clarify how difficult the problem is.** The distance between the problem state and the exact goal state gives the problem solver a sense of the effort required to solve the problem.

◆ **Specific targets enable the creation of a specific solution.** If you know exactly what you want, you can create a solution path that will take you there. Another Key of Wisdom reminds us of this fact:

The more specific the goal, the more specific the solution can be.

Quantify your goals in some fashion. Criteria of quality, durability, satisfaction, and risk should be quantified, as should goals for time, cost, duration, and so forth.

5.4.2 SPECIFIC GOALS PROVIDE A TIMETABLE FOR ACTION.

Breaking an overall goal down into intermediate goals with multiple deadlines allows for the planning and organization of work for them. (See Chapter 8, Section 8.2.3, for more about this.) The act of working out a solution in the problem-solving process might be compared to the process of project management, and project management is almost defined by its use of timetables.

Setting expected dates of accomplishment for both short-term and long-term goals is important for stimulating action on those goals. In fact, yet another Key of Wisdom reminds us that due dates separate the truly expected from the imaginary:

⚿ **A goal without a completion date is wishful thinking.**

5.4.3 SPECIFIC GOALS PROVIDE A MEASURE OF PROGRESS.

One of the most common questions in the working world, "How's it going?" is actually a request for a progress report. If someone answered, "We don't know where we're going, but we're making excellent progress," the questioner would rightly think the answer was a joke. In fact, the questioner might respond with another joke—that makes a point: "How will you know when you are halfway to nowhere in particular?"

Having specific goals permits the problem solver to make regular assessments of the progress of the solution. These assessments answer the following questions.

- ◆ How much progress has been made since the last check?
- ◆ How close are we to the goal?
- ◆ What is the predicted time until the finish?
- ◆ Are we still moving toward the goal, or have we begun to move away?

Two qualifications should be made here.

- ◆ **Specific goals may need adjustment.** When the actual solution is chosen, the particulars of the solution itself may require some adjustment in time or even in the nature of the solution. For example, the goal of "painting the entire complex by June" may have to be altered if necessary surface preparation turns out to be more extensive than originally thought.
- ◆ **Progress toward some goals is not always clear.** For some problems, such as the search for a breakthrough in drug research or the testing of a new marketing plan, problem solvers sometimes believe they are making progress when they are not, or believe they are not when they are. Therefore, progress can sometimes be viewed only in hindsight once the successful solution has been found.

QUESTIONS FOR REVIEW AND DISCUSSION.

1. When a problem is clearly identified, what should be developed next?
   Ⓐ Possible goal states.
   B. Possible solution paths.

2. A management team learns that some employees are reportedly using the Internet for personal matters during business hours. One member of the team wants to eliminate personal Internet use entirely. Another member

wants to limit such use to break and lunch periods. A third member wants to permit a reasonable amount of time for personal Internet use as long as it does not interfere with work. These three team members are expressing three different

(A.) possible solution paths.
B. present states or problems.
C. possible goal states.

3. What three benefits do goals provide when used as criteria for solutions? (Answer in three short sentences.) *Keep the solution focused, measure success of sol, select best solution from other alternatives*

4. In this chapter, four types of values are mentioned. For each of the following, indicate which type of value is being expressed. Select the single, most obvious type in each case.
   (a) A management team member speaks out against what he sees as unfair and possibly deceptive (though perfectly legal) fine print in a contract for the company's services. *ethical*
   (b) Congress mandates that all new sport utility vehicles must be more fuel-efficient. *legal*
   (c) A business tries to ship all orders within 24 hours of receipt. *corporate*
   (d) A husband wants to buy a particular refrigerator because he prefers the brushed aluminum exterior; the wife wants to buy a different one with more interior room. *personal*

5. The consistency provided by a defined set of values reduces what three diminishments to problem solving? (Your answer needs only three words.) *Drift, expediency, confusion*

6. A school district wants to eliminate all cheating on tests. Would you classify this as an ideal goal or a practical goal? Explain. *ideal*

7. "Since ideal goals can seldom be achieved, considering them only gets in the way of the realities of the problem-solving process." Is this statement consistent with the material presented in this chapter? Explain.

8. At a staff meeting, the manager says, "Our goal is to reduce shoplifting." Does this goal provide a "completion test"? Explain, adding such a test if necessary.

9. According to the discussion in this chapter, does the attempt to quantify a goal (e.g., how expensive, how many hours) interfere with finding effective solutions to problems? Explain.

10. Complete this Key of Wisdom: "A goal without a completion date is
    _____ _____."

11. This statement is made near the end of the chapter: "Having specific goals
    permits the problem solver to make regular assessments of the progress of
    the solution." What two qualifications are made to this statement? (Use
    only two sentences for your answer.)

12. Suppose one of your best employees came to you and said that she believed
    she was not making any progress toward solving a problem you had as-
    signed. She has put a lot of work into it, but cannot see any results. Find a
    sentence or two from this chapter that you could quote to her in order to
    encourage her to continue working toward a solution.

_____

Chapter 6

❖

The Problem-Solving Cycle 3
Generating Ideas

The best way to have a good idea is to have a lot of ideas.
—Linus Pauling

The very idea that there is another idea is something gained.
—Richard Jefferies

The third step in the problem-solving cycle is Generating Ideas for solutions to the problem. The goal of this stage of the problem-solving process is to identify many possible solutions to the problem so that the best one or ones can be discovered.

The Problem-Solving Cycle

Exploring the Problem

Establishing Goals

➔ Generating Ideas ⬅

Choosing the Solution

Implementing the Solution

Evaluating the Solution

This chapter emphasizes the following aspects of idea generation:

- Many good ideas come from observing how similar problems have been solved.
- Comparing a problem to a familiar situation by analogy helps produce ideas for a solution.
- Breaking the problem down into parts provides a new approach to a solution.
- The classic technique of brainstorming helps generate many ideas.
- When the problem solver imaginatively changes roles, new approaches to the problem become available.

6.1 ASSOCIATIVE TECHNIQUES.

Comparing something unfamiliar (such as a problem) to something familiar is a common and powerful way to find understanding and, often, solutions. The associative techniques in this section all make use of comparison in some form:

What in the problem solver's knowledge or experience can shed light on the problem at hand? Answers may come from other problems, inventions, the natural world, or just everyday life.

6.1.1 DIRECT TRANSFER.

During the course of problem exploration discussed in Chapter 4, Section 4.1.2, it was recommended that you research the problem to discover whether it has existed in the past, and if so, how it was handled by others. If an effective solution exists, it can be applied in the present case—or at least become one of the candidates for choice in the present case.

Three of the four creative problem-solving methods discussed in Chapter 1 can be used with the direct transfer technique: Reapplication, evolution, and synthesis all involve the use of existing ideas to produce new ideas or new solutions. See Chapter 1, Section 1.3, for more information.

A starting point in the process of identifying ideas for solutions, then, is to ask the following questions:

- ◆ Has this problem been solved in the past?
- ◆ What was the solution?
- ◆ Did that solution work?
- ◆ How well did the solution work?
- ◆ Will that solution work again now or in this case?
- ◆ Is that solution the best way to solve the problem?
- ◆ If the problem has been solved before in more than one way, which way worked the best?

Each of these questions is important. A solution that worked in the past may have worked only moderately or even not at all well. Even a solution that worked well in the past may no longer work because of changes in technology, society, law, and so forth. For example, molasses with strychnine made an excellent ant poison in the 1960s, but it would be considered too dangerous to use today because of increased concern for protecting children from poisons.

Direct transfer is such a popular problem-solving method that millions of patents exist to protect unique solutions from wholesale copying by others. Nevertheless, many excellent solutions are not patented and can often be readily transferred to the situation at hand. Indeed, many solutions are borrowed directly from the natural world. The study of plants and animals provides an endless source of good ideas for problem solving.

Example 6.1.1.1

Some insect-catching plants have a trap in the form of a long tube with a sweet-smelling liquid at the bottom to attract and drown the insects. We could design a similar trap made of plastic; it could have a removable base to clean out dead insects and add fresh bait-liquid.

6.1.2 CLOSE ANALOGY.

An analogy compares two things by identifying one or more points of similarity between them. A simple example would be to say that the kidney is like a water filter, because both filter out impurities. Whether you are teaching someone else something new, or trying to learn something yourself, or trying to solve a problem, one of the best ways for doing any of these is to compare the unfamiliar, unknown, or problematic with something familiar and understandable. This is the method of analogy—often called analogical transfer—to find a familiar thing or process that seems somewhat like the idea or problem to be clarified.

Problem solving by close analogy looks within the same general area as the problem itself for a similar problem and solution that might be applied. Close analogies usually have several points of similarity.

Example 6.1.2.1

Our software company wants to write a patient-tracking program for a medical clinic so that records of services can be kept (doctors seen, diagnoses, treatments, etc.). Where else would we find similar maintenance-tracking software? What about the auto repair business, where cars and their repair history are tracked? We can get many good ideas from studying those systems.

Close analogies are easier to find when the problem solver has a thorough knowledge of the area (or *domain*) in which the problem is found.

6.1.3 REMOTE ANALOGY.

A remote analogy results when the problem is compared to something outside the problem area. Often, only one or two points of similarity exist between the problem and the thing or idea to which it is compared. In creative problem solving, remote analogies are used for their suggestive qualities to see what ideas they can break loose, and especially for helping to examine the problem better. By searching for points of similarity between the analogy and the problem, new aspects of the problem are revealed and new approaches arise. In spite of surface differences, there is at least some underlying similarity. The invention of Pringles® potato chips made use of remote analogy (see Davis, 1986, p. 109), as the following example shows:

Example 6.1.3.1

Problem: How to package fragile potato chips so they will not break during shipping.

Analogy: Potato chips are something like leaves. Dried leaves are fragile, but wet leaves are soft and can be stacked together.

Idea: Make potato chips that can be stacked and stack them together vertically in a single-stack can.

6.1.4 FORCED ANALOGY.

Both close and remote analogies are created by the problem solver's asking, "What is my problem similar to?" The goal of the thinking process is then to search creatively for some item or idea that has at least one element of similarity. Forced analogies, on the other hand, begin with the selection of an item of comparison—often arbitrarily chosen—which the problem solver must then force into similarity with the problem.

> **Example 6.1.4.1**
> Adams (1986) gives the following problem: "Assume that you have been hired as a consultant by a restaurant that is having business problems. See how many ways you can think of to improve the business of the restaurant using the concept of a runover dead cat" (p. 79).
> The question is, "How are improvements to the restaurant similar to a runover dead cat?" Here are a few "forced" similarities:
> - Cat guts, catgut, tennis racket—make the restaurant a sports club or decorate it with a sports theme or install game machines or a giant-screen TV and show sporting events.
> - Flat cat, tire tread marks, artsy in an avant-garde mode—add to the restaurant an art gallery with modern art on the walls, put in chrome and glass and high-tech furnishings. Decorated dining plus art sales.
> - Who killed the cat? Offer surprise entrées or mystery desserts.
> - Cats, catsup, the Catsup Supper Club—a burger place with white table-cloths.
> - Is the cat run over repeatedly? Build repeat business by giving a free meal, drink, or gift after nine (cat's lives) visits.

As strange as the forced analogy method may sound at first, it often works quite well. Sources of forced analogy can be lists of words (such as *lake, tree, stone, wall, shovel*), books (dictionaries, the Yellow Pages), or a stroll through a variety store.

6.2 ANALYTIC TECHNIQUES.

The analytic techniques for generating ideas involve manipulating the problem by breaking it down, turning it around, or distributing it to many others. In each case, the problem is viewed in a new way (or by a new person), yielding new possibilities for solution.

6.2.1 ATTRIBUTE ANALYSIS.

Attribute analysis is the process of breaking down a problem into attributes, qualities, or component parts and then working with individual attributes rather than the problem as a whole.

- **List the attributes** or qualities of the problem by analyzing its structure.
- **List many alternatives** for each attribute in a column beneath.
- **Choose alternatives** from each column. You can perform a deliberate analysis of each alternative or choose a random alternative from each column and assemble the choices into a possibility for a new idea. Repeat as many times as you wish.

Example 6.2.1.1

Problem: Develop a better bandage.

What are the current attributes of a bandage? In the table below, the attributes are listed in the first row, current forms of those attributes in the second row, and alternates in the subsequent rows.

Bandage Attribute Analysis				
Adhesion	**Color**	**Material**	**Shape**	**Pad Type**
stick on	*flesh colored*	*plastic*	*rectangular*	*gauzed*
magnetic	red or green	cloth	round	medicated
tie on	flower pattern	paper	triangular	cellulose
glue on	transparent	Tyvek®	octagon	sawdust
paint on	black	metal	square	nylon
Velcro®	words (ouch)	composite	trapezoid	plastic
clamp on	stripes	rubber	animals	cotton

Choosing only one alternative might result in paint-on bandages (a current product) or animal-shaped bandages. Choosing multiple options might result in a glue-on black paper triangular bandage with a cotton-ball pad.

6.2.2 REVERSAL.

The reversal method for generating new ideas takes a situation and turns it around, inside out, backwards, or upside down.

Example 6.2.2.1

Problem: Wine has often been aged in oak barrels to impart a special flavor characteristic. Today, in many wineries, modern processing has eliminated oak barrels in favor of stainless steel tanks. In such a situation, how can the oaky flavor be maintained?

Simple reversal: If we cannot put the wine in the oak, can we put the oak in the wine?

Solution: Put oak slices or chips into the stainless steel tanks along with the wine as it ages.

Example 6.2.2.2

A variety store chain was being hurt by the competition. Some possible reversals of "the store being hurt by the competition" include these:

♦ How can the store hurt the competition?

♦ How can competition help the store?

♦ How can the competition hurt itself?

♦ How can the store help itself?

The second reversal, "How can competition help the store?" was chosen and was implemented by sending employees to competing stores to examine displays, floor plans, goods quality and selection, anything that appeared to be effective or useful. The employees brought these ideas back and implemented the best of them. The result was that the competition did help the store.

A given situation can be reversed in several ways; there is no single method. Each reversal can be analyzed for useful ideas. The reversal itself should form a stimulus for thought, even if it is not useful or practical by itself. In the example below, note the possible practical ideas suggested by each reversal.

Example 6.2.2.3

Problem: How can the situation, "a teacher instructing students," be improved by reversal?

♦ Students instructing the teacher. (Students do research and give reports or teach a class?)

♦ The teacher uninstructing students. (Teacher correcting misconceptions about the subject by students?)

♦ Students instructing themselves. (Guided workbook, better homework?)

♦ Students instructing each other. (Use of teams, study groups, joint papers?)

♦ Teacher instructing himself or herself. (Freshen course material, read journals in field, study instructional methods?)

♦ Students uninstructing (correcting?) the teacher. (Teacher presents urban legends that students must research and correct?)

In some reversals, ideas are generated, which then can be reversed again into ideas applicable to the original problem.

Example 6.2.2.4

Problem: How can management improve the store?

Reversal: How can management hurt the store?

♦ Charge high prices on low-quality goods.

♦ Keep the floors dirty.

♦ Be rude to customers.

♦ Hire careless employees.

Re-reversals (with some possible ideas):

♦ Charge low prices on high-quality goods. (Sell upscale merchandise at discount?)

♦ Keep the floors clean. (Start a new cleaning schedule?)

♦ Be polite to customers. (Provide employee training for "touch, speak, smile" behavior?)

♦ Hire careful employees. (Implement better employment screening?)

Re-reversals can be effective because it is sometimes easier to think negatively first and then reverse the negatives.

6.2.3 PUBLIC SOLUTION.

The most powerful computers contain not one but several CPUs (central processing units) so that they can perform parallel processing—processing several sets of information at one time. The use of the public solution method of idea generation imitates this multiplicity by recruiting many people into the solution-seeking process. Several minds begin to work on the problem, both independently and in discussion with others, resulting in fresh possibilities.

To use this technique, post the problem on a bulletin board or Web page, circulate it in a memo or newsletter, send it out by e-mail, or use an e-mail listserve. If you have developed more than one description of the problem, you may choose to circulate those different versions to ensure some different approaches to solutions.

6.3 CREATIVE QUESTIONS.

A fruitful method of generating many ideas is to ask and answer questions about the problem.

6.3.1 MULTIDIRECTIONAL WHY.

You may have been around young children whose favorite question is "Why?" In fact, "Why?" is one of the most powerful questions in problem solving. It can clarify the problem, identify goals, and, as used here, develop possible solution ideas.

♦ **Parallel Why.** Here, "Why?" is asked of the same question over and over again, either of the same person, who must then give several different answers, or of different people, each of whom might give a unique answer. This technique generates multiple approaches to an answer.

Example 6.3.1.1

Problem: Our industrial mercury vapor light bulbs are breaking too often during shipping. Ask someone, "Why are they breaking so often?" Answer: "Our packaging is designed for a lighter weight bulb." Ask someone else, "Why are they breaking so often?" Another answer: "We changed shipping methods and the new company is too rough on them." Ask a third person, "Why are they breaking so often?" Still another answer: "We are using the wrong padding inside the box."

♦ **Serial Why.** In this questioning method, "Why?" is asked of each answer given to the previous "Why?" until the problem solver believes the avenue is exhausted. This method can be used to construct a chain of causation. (See Chapter 3, Section 3.3.4.)

Example 6.3.1.2

Problem: The company has experienced a $310 million loss this quarter. Why? Sales suddenly declined. Why? Customers turned to competitive products. Why? Our flagship product is outdated. Why? Research and development costs were cut last year. Why? —And so on.

♦ **Why Tree.** A Why Tree combines the Parallel Why and Serial Why above. A question is asked, and the multiple answers to the "Why?" are listed. Then, "Why?" is asked of each of those answers, with multiple responses given to each. The process continues with each of those responses.

6.3.2 MANIPULATIVE VERBS.

Verbs are the action words of the language; they tell us what something is doing or how to perform an activity. As agents of action, verbs can provide great stimulation for idea discovery.

Example 6.3.2.1

Problem: How to improve a table. The manipulative verb is *inflate*. Creative question: How can a table be inflated? Make the table larger, floating, of inflated vinyl, with thick top and legs, with a high price to cater to upscale consumers, with air vents in the table to blow out cool or heated air or to suck in smoke from cigarettes.

There are two categories of manipulative verbs.

♦ **Standard alterations.** These are verbs that suggest commonly used ways of altering a problem situation or thing to produce a new perspective or new ideas.

Standard Alteration Manipulative Verbs		
enlarge	combine	subtract
reduce	divide	rearrange
replace	add	multiply

♦ **Custom alterations.** These verbs suggest an unusual way of altering the problem situation. One or more of them can be chosen either at random or because of a perceived appropriateness. The list is nearly endless. The table below contains just a few examples.

Example Custom Alteration Manipulative Verbs		
freeze	crush	rotate
heat	bend	transpose
melt	inflate	display
loosen	stretch	submerge
twist	invert	automate

6.3.3 PREPOSITIONS.

Creative questions can also be generated using prepositions, those words that indicate direction: *across, into, through, over, under, around, between,* and so forth.

Example 6.3.3.1

Problem: Our meetings last too long and we don't get enough done. How can we increase our efficiency? Prepositional question: What does going *between* the meeting suggest? Subcommittees, breaks, divide them into shorter mini-meetings, interrupt them for points of order. What about *under* the meeting? A reward for using less than the allotted time, better foundation work or research to bring to the meeting, bring to the surface underlying motives for delay.

6.4 BRAINSTORMING.

Brainstorming is a classic technique invented by Osborn (1963), which is useful for attacking specific problems where fresh, new ideas are needed. For example, a specific problem such as how to mark the content of pipes (water, steam, etc.) would lend itself to brainstorming much better than a more general problem such as how the educational system can be improved. Note, though, that even general problems can be submitted to brainstorming with success.

Brainstorming can take place either individually or in a group of two to ten, with four to seven being ideal.

6.4.1 BRAINSTORMING GUIDELINES.

The four guidelines of brainstorming were established to keep the process from freezing up, either from a lack of bold creativity or from premature criticism.

♦ **Suspend judgment.** This is the most important guideline. When ideas are brought forth, no critical comments are allowed. *All* ideas are written down. Evaluation is reserved for later. The temptation to be instantly critical or analytic must be resisted.

♦ **Think freely.** Freewheeling, wild, impossible ideas are fine. Remember that practical ideas very often come from silly, impractical, impossible ones. By permitting yourself to think outside the boundaries of ordinary, normal thought, brilliant new solutions can arise. Some ideas thought at first to be wildly impractical turn out to be quite practical after all.

Example 6.4.1.1

When the subway was being dug under Victoria station in London, water began seeping in. What are the ways to remedy this? Pumps, or liners of steel or concrete? While thinking freely, someone suggested freezing it. That wild idea became the solution. Horizontal holes were drilled into the wet soil and liquid nitrogen was pumped in, freezing the water until the tunnel could be dug and cemented.

♦ **Tag on.** Improve, modify, or build on the ideas of others. What is good about the idea just suggested? How can it be made to work? What changes would make it better or even wilder? Tagging on is sometimes called piggybacking, hitchhiking, or ping-ponging. Changing just one aspect of an unworkable solution can sometimes make it a great solution.

♦ **Quantity of ideas is important.** Concentrate on generating a large stock of ideas for later evaluation. There are two reasons for desiring a large quantity. First, the obvious ideas seem to come to mind most readily, so that the first dozen or two ideas are probably not going to be fresh and creative. Second, the larger your list of possibilities, the more you will have to choose from, adapt, or combine.

6.4.2 PRACTICAL CONSIDERATIONS FOR BRAINSTORMING.

Brainstorming sessions work more effectively if a few practical rules are followed.

♦ **Record the ideas.** Someone should be put in charge of writing down all the ideas, preferably on a board or large sheets of paper on the walls so that the group can see them. For a one-person brainstorming session, using a large piece of paper (such as 11" x 17") is useful.

♦ **Use a moderator.** For groups of more than three or four, use a moderator to choose who will offer an idea next, so that several people do not speak at once. The moderator should call on those with ideas that tag onto previous ideas, then call on those with new ideas. If necessary, the moderator will also remind members of the group not to inject evaluation into the session.

- **Keep the session relaxed and playful.** The creative juices flow best when participants are relaxed, enjoying themselves, and feeling free to be silly or playful. Eat popcorn or make paper airplanes or doodle while you work, even if the problem itself is deadly serious.
- **Try a warm-up session.** As an aid to relaxation and a stimulation to creativity, it is often useful to begin with a ten-minute warm-up session where an imaginary problem is tackled, such as how to light a house with a single light bulb.
- **Limit the session.** A typical session should be limited to about fifteen to thirty minutes. Experienced brainstormers sometimes have an hour-long session.
- **Make copies.** After the session, type up the list and make copies for each member of the group. No attempt should be made to put the list in any particular order.
- **Add and evaluate.** The group should meet again the next day. First, ideas thought of since the previous session should be shared and added to the photocopied lists. Then the group should evaluate each of the ideas for their potential to be developed as practical solutions.

6.4.3 STEPPING STONES.

Some ideas may not be useful, practical, or realistic in themselves, but they can suggest other ideas that are. Such impractical ideas serve as stepping stones—pathways between one mental location and another. The effectiveness of stepping stones explains why so much emphasis is put on deferring judgment during brainstorming. The mind has an amazing ability to convert strange ideas into practical ones. During the evaluation session after brainstorming, wild and ridiculous ideas are converted into realistic ones or used to suggest realistic solutions. If those wild ideas had been condemned immediately, they would be unavailable for further use.

6.5 ROLE PLAYING.

Role playing consists of several techniques, having in common the use of the mind to imagine a different reality for the problem solver, to change a current state into a desired state.

6.5.1 MENTAL PRACTICE.

Mental practice is the process of working on a problem or performing in some way *in your imagination* before actually engaging in the actual activity. It is well known that many athletes rehearse their upcoming performances mentally to gain confidence and familiarity with the moment of performance. It is less well known that surgeons, attorneys, instructors, and others also use mental practice to improve the quality of their actions.

You can use mental practice in problem solving as a visualization technique, imagining yourself approaching, working on, and solving the problem.

6.5.2 BECOMING SOMEONE ELSE.

Another form of role playing is to imagine that you are someone else—someone who would know how to solve the problem. Imagine that you are an expert in the problem area. With your special knowledge, what do you know and what can you do?

Example 6.5.2.1

Problem: Design a new impeller for a water pump. What would Leonardo da Vinci do? (You may need to read his notebooks or do some other research to get a feel for his methods.) Pretend you are Leonardo. What do you do first?

A second form of becoming someone else is to change roles to see how the problem would be approached by those from different knowledge domains or areas of expertise.

Example 6.5.2.2

Suppose you must build a canal. Imagine first that you are not a canal builder but a pipeline maker. How would he or she build the canal? (Perhaps by using reinforced half-pipeline sections?) Now imagine that you are a tunnel maker. Now how would you solve the problem? (Perhaps by using an inverted tunnel?) Now imagine that you are a swimming pool builder. How would you solve it? (Perhaps by using steel reinforcing bars and sprayed-on concrete?)

6.5.3 MENTAL METAMORPHOSIS.

In this kind of role playing, you change yourself into the problem object, such as becoming a trash can ("Why don't people use me?"), a helicopter, an electric current, a germ. Notice that this technique involves turning yourself into something not human.

Example 6.5.3.1

Michael Faraday imagined that he was an atom under pressure and thereby developed his electromagnetic theory.

Example 6.5.3.2

Imagine you are a ball bearing. What do you like? (Grease?) What are you afraid of? (Sand?) What will make you live a long time? (Not being overloaded?) How can you inform someone if you are being overloaded? This last question may suggest an innovation that would provide a warning when the bearing was loaded too heavily.

QUESTIONS FOR REVIEW AND DISCUSSION.

1. In each case below, decide whether the associative technique used is direct transfer, close analogy, remote analogy, or forced analogy.
   (a) Dreaming about circling snakes provides the insight that the elements of the chemical benzene can be represented by a ring-shaped structure. *remote*
   (b) Copying an old bottle-sealing technique for a new bottle design. *direct transfer*
   (c) Solving a hospital infection problem by arbitrarily comparing it to playing tennis. *forced*
   (d) Getting an idea for a new camera lens by examining a microscope lens. *close*

2. True or *False:* The direct transfer associative technique must always involve two similar manufactured technologies. *could be material, just direct transfer as technologies is necessary*

3. *True* or False: For forced analogy to work, it is not necessary for the problem and the compared thing to have any obvious similarities at first.

4. The analytic technique that breaks the problem into component parts is
   A. reversal.
   B. attribute analysis.
   C. public solution.

5. To say that a reversal "should form a stimulus for thought, even though it is not itself useful or practical" is to describe a reversal as a possible
   A. analogy.
   B. attribute.
   C. stepping stone.

6. A Why Tree combines what two types of Why questioning?

7. Action words (such as *combine* or *divide*) that require the problem solver to act imaginatively on the problem are called _____ _____.

8. What are the four guidelines for a brainstorming session?

9. When you are brainstorming for new ideas, when should analysis take place to determine which ideas are good and which are not?

10. Which form of role playing involves becoming something not human?

Example 2.1.2.1 Solved

Here are a few ways to solve the problem presented in Example 2.1.2.1 in Chapter 2, page 13:

1. Carefully cut along the dotted lines as shown in the left-hand illustration below. The middle will then expand into a hole.
2. Cut two parallel spirals as shown in the middle illustration below. Again, the middle will then expand into a hole.
3. Cut a slit in the card and push a picture of your head through the slit as shown in the third illustration below.
4. Soak the card in water to soften the fibers. Then, run the card through a high-pressure rolling mill, turning it 90 degrees after each pass. The card will be ironed out large enough to cut a head-sized hole in the middle.
5. Cut the card into a single large spiral and tape the two ends together to form the hole.

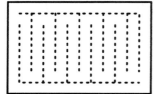  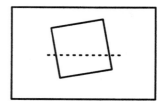

Chapter 7

The Problem-Solving Cycle 4
Choosing the Solution

Quick decisions are unsafe decisions.
—Sophocles

To choose, it is first necessary to know.
—Herman Finer

In the fourth step of the problem-solving cycle, a solution is chosen from among the possibilities identified during the idea-generating step.

```
The Problem-Solving Cycle
Exploring the Problem
Establishing Goals
Generating Ideas
→ Choosing the Solution ←
Implementing the Solution
Evaluating the Solution
```

This chapter emphasizes the following aspects of choosing a solution:
- Before any choices are made, know what type of solution is desired.
- A solution provides a pathway to a goal.
- Both intended and unintended consequences of each solution should be taken into account.
- Consider effectiveness, efficiency, and simplicity in making a selection.

7.1 WHAT IS A SOLUTION?

In our ordinary discourse, we often think of "solving a problem" in the sense of making it go away, so that the problem no longer exists. This indeed is one kind of solution, but it is not the only kind. Some problems cannot be eliminated entirely: We are never likely to eliminate trash and its challenges, or the wear on automobile tires, or the occurrence of illness. We can, however, create solutions or treatments that will lessen each of these problems.

7.1.1 DEFINITION.

You may recall from the discussions in Chapters 2 and 3 that a problem might be thought of as the difference between a current state and a goal state. By extension, then, a solution might be thought of as a method or an activity that moves the problem state to the goal state. In other words, we can define a solution as follows:

A **solution** is the management of a problem in a way that meets the goals established for it.

The possibilities inherent in the problem, together with the ambitiousness, resources, and values of the problem solver, will help shape the goals. When the goals have been established, then a solution can be chosen that matches the goals as closely as possible. Sometimes the goal will be to eliminate the problem entirely; sometimes the goal will be only to reduce the effects of the problem.

7.1.2 APPROACHES TO SOLUTIONS.

When a problem is attacked at its source, a solution may be chosen to stop or eliminate the problem altogether. When only the symptoms of a problem are treated, the solution merely mops up the effects of the problem. We can therefore speak of stop-it and mop-it kinds of solutions.

To illustrate how these solutions differ—how each one will aim at a different goal—we will use the same problem for each one, described in the following example:

> **Example 7.1.2.1**
>
> The manager of an older hotel comes to work one morning and is told that the central water heater has begun to leak, and water is trickling out into the lobby. What should be done?

7.2 STOP-IT SOLUTIONS.

A stop-it approach is designed to cure a problem, so that, insofar as possible, the problem no longer exists. Its three forms are prevention, elimination, and reduction.

7.2.1 PREVENT IT.

By preventing a problem from occurring (or recurring) we have perhaps the ideal solution. In the water heater example, the manager might have scheduled regular maintenance on the water heater (such as replacing the lining that some of them have). The prevention approach is often a difficult one to apply because it requires predictive foresight ("This might be a problem someday if we do not act now"), and it is often costly. And, of course, many problems occur unexpectedly and in spite of the best foresight.

The prevent-it approach might be seen as a proactive solution or a solution in advance of a problem, designed to eliminate a problem before it occurs. For example, if you can prevent a cold or an automobile accident or a crime, you will not have to deal any further with a problem or its effects. Similarly, by preventing misunderstandings in communication, the need to correct wrongly assembled parts or misdirected memos can be avoided.

7.2.2 ELIMINATE IT.

Eliminating a problem once and for all is also an excellent way of attacking a problem. In the leaking water heater example, an elimination solution would be to repair the leak that caused the problem (all that water on the floor) or even replace the water heater with a new one. Elimination solutions should be considered in nearly every problem situation.

Example 7.2.2.1

A resident of a mountainous semirural area had chronic trouble getting suitable TV reception. Every weekend he was on his roof installing another antenna (he eventually had three), rotating one, putting another up on a higher mast, and so on. He finally eliminated the problem by subscribing to cable TV.

7.2.3 REDUCE IT.

As we mentioned earlier, some problems, like trash production, cannot be eliminated entirely. In such cases, a strategy of reduction can be highly effective. Almost any problem can be made less troublesome by reducing its size. In the water heater example, suppose the manager could not obtain a repair (an elimination solution) until a day or two later. Until then, the problem might be reduced by turning off the incoming water. Without line pressure on the tank, the leak would slow down; that would be better than a full-force leak.

Example 7.2.3.1

Current approaches to the flow of illegal drugs into the United States include reduction strategies. The flow of drugs cannot be eliminated as long as demand continues, so solving the problem focuses on reducing both the supply and the demand as much as possible.

7.3 MOP-IT SOLUTIONS.

A mop-it approach focuses on treating the effects of a problem. As you can guess, the name comes from the leaking water heater example. Instead of treating the leak itself, the manager will have the water on the floor—the effects caused by the problem—mopped up.

7.3.1 TREAT IT.

Here the damage caused by the problem is repaired or treated. We mop up the water, fix the damaged floor, hang the rugs out to dry. Note two things: (1) by itself, a treat-it solution is not going to be nearly as effective as some form of stop-it solution, and (2) treat-it solutions are often needed in addition to an elimination or reduction form of solution.

Example 7.3.1.1

When a termite infestation is discovered in a building, the owners are often faced with the choice between an eliminate-it solution (tenting and gassing the entire building) and a treat-it solution (local spraying). The cost difference is substantial, but sometimes, so is the difference in ultimate effectiveness.

7.3.2 TOLERATE IT.

In this form of mop-it approach, the effects of the problem are tolerated. In the leaky water heater example, the manager might have a drain installed in the floor, or waterproof the floor. The effects are taken for granted and measures are taken to endure them.

Example 7.3.2.1

Vandalism is now taken for granted in many large cities, so tolerance measures have been implemented, such as installing new lighting or landscaping that is more difficult to destroy or less expensive to replace.

The tolerate-it approach is taken when the problem appears to be so large or entrenched that other approaches appear unlikely to work.

7.3.3 REDIRECT IT.

This approach to problem solving involves deflecting the problem. In the case of the leaking water heater, the manager might decide that the problem belongs to the water heater manufacturer and demand that the manufacturer repair the heater and mop up the floor.

Example 7.3.3.1

Some police departments have been known to buy bus or airline tickets for chronic offenders (prostitutes, usually) to send them to another state far across the country, thus "solving" the local problem.

Delegating a problem to a subordinate or a committee is a popular form of redirection in problem solving. So is transferring blame: Many lawsuits involve the issue of determining who is responsible for a particular problem; in other words, lawsuits are often attempts to use the redirection method of problem solving.

Stop-it, Mop-it, and Stop-gap

Sometimes a mop-it solution is all that is available. For example, when you get a cold, there is no elimination solution that works. In general, however, be careful to investigate the possibility of implementing a stop-it solution before you fall back to mop-it ones. There is a temptation to focus on symptomatic treatments for problems when we should be looking for treatments of the underlying causes.

Mop-it solutions often serve as effective stop-gap measures. These temporary actions reduce the worst immediate effects of a problem by controlling the symptoms until the root cause of the problem can be addressed.

7.4 SOLUTION PATHS

If you have been reading the chapters of this book in order, you have already learned some things about solutions paths:

- **The goal is more important than the path.** The Key of Wisdom in Chapter 1 informs us, "The goal is to solve the problem, not to implement a particular solution." It is important to be on guard against path fixation (Chapter 1, Section 1.3.4).

- **Different goals will require different paths.** Establishing one or more clear goals helps determine which solution path to choose (Chapter 5, Section 5.1.1).

7.4.1 THE SOLUTION PATH MAY CONTAIN MORE THAN ONE ACTIVITY.

The idea of a solution as a pathway might be extended to say that a solution is a road or highway over which one *or more* solution activities move the problem state to the goal state:

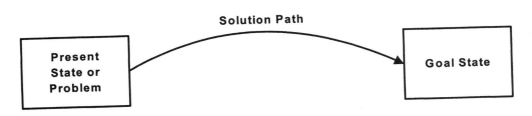

From Present State to Goal State Over the Solution Path

It is important to note that a solution to a problem will often consist of a bundle of activities rather than a single one. During the idea-generation phase of the cycle (discussed in Chapter 6), many possible solutions may have been identified for a given problem. It would be a mistake to believe that only one of them must be chosen. To use an image common in the software industry, problem solving often involves *a suite of solutions* (that is, a set of solutions). When you think about the diagram on the previous page, then, be sure to view the solution-path line as a road with many vehicles (the solution activities) on it.

Example 7.4.1.1

The solution path to the leaky water heater problem discussed above might include (1) mopping the floor, (2) patching the leak, (3) performing some maintenance to prevent future leaks, (4) installing a drain, and (5) building a water dam along the floor to keep any future leaking water out of the lobby before it can run down the drain. Together these solutions constitute a suite or set.

7.4.2 MANY PROBLEMS CAN BE SOLVED IN MORE THAN ONE WAY.

One of the benefits of idea generation is to break the problem solver out of a search for *the* solution. The question to be asked instead is, "What are some solutions?" As a result, it may be that several ways of solving the problem exist, any one of which will reach the desired goal state. A diagram like the one below might represent such a case:

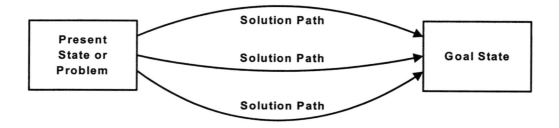

Alternative Solution Paths to the Goal State

In this case, the decision is not which combination of solution activities on a single solution path will best achieve the goal state, but which alternative path (each made up of an activity or a set of activities) will do so.

7.5 CONSEQUENCE ANALYSIS.

Whether you will be selecting solution activities for a single path or choosing from among several solution paths, it is desirable to know as much as possible about the consequences of each solution. Consequence analysis is an important step in the idea-selection process.

7.5.1 SOLUTIONS AS PROBLEMS.

Knowing only which solution will eliminate the problem is not enough because solutions often have consequences unrelated to the problem. In fact, the consequences may themselves be troublesome, as this Key of Wisdom reminds us:

⚷ **The solution to one problem is often the cause of another problem.**

Consequence analysis is the identification of possible consequences caused by (1) solving the problem and (2) using a particular solution path to do so. Both positive and negative consequences should be identified so that a realistic assessment of benefits and costs can be made.

For illustrating the three types of consequences discussed below, we will use a single example:

Example 7.5.1.1

Problem: The Yangtze River in China is subject to recurrent, devastating flooding. There is also a need for more electricity to power China's growing industrial base.

Solution: Build the Three Gorges hydroelectric dam across the river.

7.5.2 DIRECT AND INDIRECT CONSEQUENCES.

Many times, a solution acts not only on the problem itself but has some other effect as well. The secondary effect may be indirect—that is, the solution may set in motion a chain of events that ultimately results in further consequences. Indirect consequences, like direct ones, can be either positive or negative. Indeed, the prospect of indirect benefits may be one of the deciding factors in choosing a particular solution.

In the Three Gorges example, a direct consequence and benefit is the economic strength given to the Chinese construction industry. An indirect consequence might be the impact on world financial markets of the estimated 25 billion dollars in borrowing needed to build the dam.

Unfortunately, unforeseen indirect consequences sometimes appear long after the solution has been implemented.

Example 7.5.2.1

At the intersection of a busy road and a more moderately traveled road, the city altered the timing of the traffic signals to allow the drivers on the busy road a longer green light. The direct consequence was better flow of cars on the busy road. Eventually, however, many of the drivers on the moderately traveled road, having tired of their long waits, grew reckless and began to run the red lights.

7.5.3 PHYSICAL AND SOCIAL CONSEQUENCES.

The physical consequences of a solution, such as what it costs or how much it saves, can often be seen and measured with a little thought and effort. The social consequences, however, are sometimes not as apparent. Measuring the amount of increased or reduced stress generated by a solution, for example, may be difficult.

The physical consequences of the Three Gorges dam will include reduced flooding downstream and 18,000 megawatts of hydroelectric power, as well as the disappearance of some forest, archaeological sites and even villages (all of which will be inundated by the 370-mile lake behind the dam). Note that these consequences are quantifiable in some respects, at least.

The social consequences will include a feeling of more safety from flooding, as well as the stress caused by the relocation of two million people whose land and homes will be flooded by the lake. Note that these effects are more subjective and more challenging to measure.

As you will learn more about in the next chapter, a critical requirement of the best, successful solutions is that they be acceptable to those involved with them. For this reason, consider carefully the social impact—the social response—of each solution candidate in addition to its effectiveness otherwise. A critical Key of Wisdom warns us of the danger:

A solution that is technologically brilliant but sociologically stupid will not work.

Example 7.5.3.1

Common experience reveals that the lines outside women's restrooms in stadiums and theaters are almost always longer than those outside men's. Someone analyzed the problem, determined that the crux was sitting time versus standing time, and invented a plastic funnel that would allow women to urinate standing up. The technology worked, but the sociology did not; hence, the restroom waiting problem was not solved by that invention.

7.5.4 SHORT-TERM AND LONG-TERM CONSEQUENCES.

Failure to look far down the road when thinking about solutions sometimes causes "quick fix" solutions to explode with unforeseen (and, of course, unintended) long-term, harmful consequences. The future is not predictable with certainty, but giving some thought to the long-term potential effects of each solution candidate should at least be included in the decision process.

The Three Gorges dam is expected to increase shipping on the Yangtze River in the short term, by making the waterway easier to navigate. There are concerns, however, that in the long term, at least some ports will become clogged with the silt that can no longer wash down the river.

Example 7.5.4.1

During World War II, DDT was used heavily to kill lice. Thousands of people were blasted with the powder, effectively handling the lice problem. Years later, however, DDT was implicated in the decline of some species of birds because the pesticide caused their eggshells to break easily, killing the chicks.

7.6 SELECTION.

Now that you have established appropriate, practical goals and their related criteria (Chapter 5), generated a number of possible solution ideas (Chapter 6), and thought about the type of solution you want to implement (Chapter 7, above), you are ready to make a selection.

7.6.1 EVALUATE THE POSSIBILITIES AND RANK THEM.

Look over each solution candidate and determine how well each one measures up according to the following standards:

- **Effectiveness.** Because true effectiveness can be measured only after a solution is implemented, this test is for *potential* effectiveness. Another way to describe this is *criteria matching.* How fully does each solution possibility match each of the criteria established for the solution? This is a test of the potential for achieving the goals you have outlined for the solution.
- **Efficiency.** How does each solution candidate rate in terms of cost-benefit analysis? That is, which candidates provide the most benefit for the least cost? Consequence analysis (Section 7.5, above) should be included in the thinking here.
- **Simplicity.** If two solution candidates are otherwise similar in their effectiveness and efficiency, the one with the simpler qualities should usually be preferred. More complex solutions present more opportunities for unforeseen complications and failures than do simple ones. In addition, implementing a simpler solution is nearly always easier.

Using these standards, rank-order each possible solution on a scale, assigning number 1 to the best, 2 to the next best, and so on.

7.6.2 CHOOSE ONE OR MORE SOLUTIONS.

From your rank-ordered list, choose the solution or solution set that appears best suited to the problem. The choice(s) will usually come from the top or near the top of the list, but sometimes subjective factors or factors not accounted for in the ranking will result in the selection of a candidate somewhat down the list.

7.6.3 IDENTIFY PLAN B.

Thinking ahead for a moment, suppose your chosen solution is a complete failure, leaving the problem the same as before (or even worse). If the problem has some time urgency, as many do, you will not want to begin the entire problem-solving cycle over again. Therefore, while the problem-solving process is fresh in mind, select a second possibility or set (in addition to your chosen solution) to be tried if the first choice does not work (and cannot be revised to work).

7.6.4 USE CRITICISM AND SUGGESTION.

During the problem-exploration step of the problem-solving cycle, discussing the problem with others was suggested as a technique for getting further insights into the problem. A similar technique is fruitful for refining chosen solution candidates.

Making use of the observations of critics to improve a plan or idea is not often used simply because most people do not like criticism. Our ideas are our precious children; to be told that they are ugly or defective can be painful and offensive. However, it is possible to work around the ego sensitivity by refocusing our *criticism seeking* into *suggestion seeking* and by viewing the procedure as a formal technique for exploiting the minds, experiences, and ideas of other people. Here are some guidelines to follow:

- **Choose in advance a fixed number of people** you will talk to, to reduce fear and make the process more formulaic (which will make it less ego damaging). Four to six is usually a good number.
- **Frame your request for criticism in a positive way**, so that the criticizer will have to suggest improvements rather than just point out defects. For example, "I have an idea to sell concentrated or dehydrated apple juice. Can you think of some ways to improve it?"
- **Ask for an analysis of defects or inadequacies.** When you get more confidence, ask for negative criticism, but still include a request for an improvement, not just condemnation. For example, "What am I missing? What am I not thinking of? What am I not taking into account?"

Another possibility is to ask various people to improve the original proposed solution, incorporate their suggestions into the proposal, and then present the new idea to others for suggestion and criticism.

During this process, remember that those making suggestions may not be aware of the goals, constraints, and other factors that have led you to your chosen solution. Do not be surprised, then, if others make some suggestions that you have already rejected or that do not conform to the goals you have identified.

QUESTIONS FOR REVIEW AND DISCUSSION.

1. A solution can be thought of as
   A. effective problem management.
   B. meeting goals established for treating a problem.
   C. both A and B.
   D. neither A nor B.

2. Ideally, the best type of stop-it solution is
   A. eliminate it.
   B. reduce it.
   C. prevent it.

3. Treating the symptoms of a problem until the root problem itself can be engaged would be a
   A. stop-it approach.
   B. stop-gap approach.
   C. tolerate-it approach.

4. A solution path
   A. will always involve a single solution activity.
   B. may include several solution activities.
   C. is more important than the goal state.

5. Your team is faced with the problem of moving crude oil from a drilling rig to a refinery on shore. One member suggests using a long, sea-floor pipeline. Another suggests loading tanker ships at the rig and carrying the oil to the refinery. These different ideas represent
   A. different problem states.
   B. different goal states.
   C. different solution paths.

6. What are the types of consequences that may be involved in implementing a solution? (List three pairs.)

7. A positive way to include criticism in your solution analysis is to
   A. pretend the problem belongs to someone else.
   B. ask for improvement suggestions, not just negative comments.
   C. criticize the criticisms themselves.

8. Match each standard for evaluation with the idea or clue that fits it the best:

A. effectiveness   _____ fewer unforeseen complications

B. efficiency   _____ criteria matching

C. simplicity   _____ cost-benefit analysis

Chapter 8

❖

The Problem-Solving Cycle 5
Implementing the Solution

A failure to consult others who have a stake in our decisions is
often seen as an act of aggression, because it often is.
—Russell L. Ackoff

People aren't in the market for solutions to problems they don't
see, acknowledge, and understand.
—William Bridges

This chapter covers the fifth step in the problem-solving cycle, Implementing the Solution.

```
The Problem-Solving Cycle
        Exploring the Problem
        Establishing Goals
        Generating Ideas
        Choosing the Solution
    →  Implementing the Solution  ←
        Evaluating the Solution
```

This chapter emphasizes the following aspects of Implementing the Solution:
- To be successful, a solution must be acceptable to those it involves.
- The appropriate type of implementation should be chosen carefully.
- Implementations are governed by plans and timelines.
- Many solutions require adjustment during implementation.

8.1 ACCEPTANCE AND THE MANAGEMENT OF CHANGE.

Implementing a solution involves both people and change. People are partly emotional beings and change can be frightening. A successful implementation of a solution must take into account the human factors connected with the situation.

8.1.1 THE HUMAN FACE OF ACCEPTANCE.

Whatever the solution you are implementing, whether a new bug spray, an employee reorganization, or a method for reducing bicycle accidents, people will nearly always be involved. Such a fact may appear obvious, but sometimes the creators of the solution become so caught up in the technical aspects of their solution that they forget this Key of Wisdom:

Almost all solutions to problems are in some way about people.

If a solution is to be implemented successfully, the people involved must accept it. The solution's users, implementers, recipients, and bystanders are all people affected by the solution.

- **Physical constraints.** Human limits of strength, endurance, eyesight, and so forth must be taken into account during the implementation process. Technology often has the capacity to exceed human ability to endure it.

Example 8.1.1.1

France's high-speed TGV commuter train could accelerate and decelerate much faster than it does, but passengers would spill their drinks or be flung out of their seats.

- **Psychological constraints.** Solutions should be implemented in a way that does not overtax the limits of attention, vision, comprehension, or memory.

Example 8.1.1.2

Problem: Mounting 16-millimeter film onto a projector was always a challenge because of the many turns and loops required. When it came time to put motion pictures on tape for home viewing, the complexity of mounting the tape was an issue. Playing a tape had to be simple if VCRs were to become popular. Solution: Put the tape into a cassette and design a mechanism to mount the tape on the transport mechanism automatically.

- **Emotional constraints.** It is not enough for those affected by a solution to accept it intellectually; they must accept it emotionally as well. People who do not feel good about a solution will often not use it. Emotional rejection is another way of describing the result of a "sociologically stupid" solution such as that discussed in Example 7.5.3.1 in the previous chapter. Similarly, if the TGV train mentioned above were to accelerate and decelerate in a high-performance manner, leaving passengers jostled and nervous rather than relaxed and calm, their emotional rejection would be understandable and ridership would likely go down.

Sometimes, however, the emotional factors are more subtle, though still significant, as the following example reveals:

Example 8.1.1.3

Years ago when cake mixes first came on the market, manufacturers put all the necessary ingredients into the mix. Only water had to be added. However, the mixes did not sell well because their consumers—primarily married women, often with children—felt guilty using them. After all, making a cake was a symbol of love for family and making a cake with hardly any work seemed like cheating. The solution was to take the egg and sometimes the milk or the oil out of the mix so that the consumers would have to participate in making the cake (while the convenience was reduced only slightly). Cake mixes with the new formula became quite popular.

As this example reveals, the technology of the implementation may need to be adjusted in order to make the solution more acceptable. In this case, while the new solution was less efficient in technical terms, it was much more acceptable to the consumers affected by it.

8.1.2 WORK TO CREATE ACCEPTANCE.

As we have seen by some of the examples above, new solutions often require new thinking to accompany them if the solutions are to be effectively implemented. The current situation is a known, while change involves the unknown and is therefore frightening for some people. Change often involves a clear loss (the previous way of doing things, the familiar software, or good coworkers), while exactly what is being gained is less clear. The challenge this creates is summed up in the following Key of Wisdom:

Fear of loss is more powerful than hope of gain.

Unless steps are taken to create acceptance, a new solution may be rejected largely because the familiar known is more comfortable than the promised, but unknown, future.

In the rapid and wrenching changes that take place in high technology, analysts sometimes speak of the FUD factor—the fear, uncertainty, and doubt that surround rumors of new products and technologies. Working toward acceptance might be seen as the process of reducing the FUD factor, by providing appropriate information and reassurances related to the solution.

Here are some ways to reduce the FUD factor and help create acceptance for a new solution:

♦ **Publicize the reasons for the change.** Instead of announcing, "Here is a new solution," or "Do this from now on," solution designers should provide a rationale for the implementation. Changes should be justified by a presentation of reasons and benefits.

- **Connect the change to the goals and values of the organization.** Show how the solution fits in with what the organization (or users of the solution) value or believe. Explain how this change makes sense as an integral part of the entire organizational system.
- **Supply a personal benefit.** Acceptance of the new can often be made easier if those affected by the change can see a benefit for themselves. "What's in it for me?" is not an uncommon question in the face of change. Identifying that benefit makes people feel that they were taken into account in the solution-design process.

Example 8.1.2.1

Increasing enrollment at a high school caused the lunchroom to become very crowded. The administration decided to divide the students into two groups and institute two lunch periods. Rather than simply announcing, "There are now two lunch periods," the administration explained that the solution would benefit the students: The dining room would be much less crowded, and time in the food line would be reduced (giving more time for eating and talking).

- **Put the change in context.** Clarify not only what will be different but also what will remain the same. Include a time frame. A fixed amount of change to reach a specific goal by a specific time is more comfortable than an indeterminate amount of change without a definite end. Without being given some clear boundaries within which a change will occur, those affected may allow their imaginations to construct worst-case scenarios.

Example 8.1.2.2

A university committee began to discuss changes in the school's general education requirements. Soon some faculty were telling each other, "A lot of us are going to lose our jobs." Only after reassurances by the administration that the changes would not result in any layoffs were these faculty members calmed down.

All the steps above are designed to increase communication with those affected by the implementation of a solution. Lack of communication is a principal cause of lack of acceptance.

8.1.3 ADMIT THE DOWNSIDE.

Few solutions are without negative aspects. Fewer still have no risks. Those affected by a solution are well aware of these facts and will want to know the downside. If the changes involved with implementing the solution are to take place in an atmosphere of trust, you must admit the negatives involved. Those riding the sea of change will be much happier if they are given a complete picture—the benefits *and* the liabilities. Without an up-front, honest assessment of the downside of the solution, there may be talk of "sugar coating," "spin doctoring," and "something to hide," which could sabotage or at least hamper what might otherwise have been a successful solution.

Make a special effort, then, to answer the following questions:

- **What are the negative consequences of the solution?** Aside from the benefits we can enjoy, what do we have to endure?
- **What are the risks?** What happens if the solution does not work? How much harm will be done? Will the damage be disastrous?
- **What will we be losing?** The question may be more personal, "What will I be losing by this?"

8.2 SOLUTION IMPLEMENTATION PLANS.

Develop a practical plan for implementing the solution. Here are some ideas:

8.2.1 IMPLEMENTATION DESIGN.

A useful way to design a plan for implementing the solution is to use the "Journalistic Six" questions: Who? What? When? Where? How? and Why? (The questions can be asked in any order.) Here are some sample questions that might be asked using this model for structuring the implementation:

- **What?** What type of implementation will be used? (See Section 8.2.2 below.) What steps are involved? What resources are available?
- **How?** How much will this cost? How will it be accomplished? How will progress be measured?
- **Why?** Why is this being done? Why is this a better solution and implementation than some other?
- **When?** When will each step be accomplished? When will the implementation begin? When will it finish? (See Section 8.2.3 below.)
- **Who?** Who are the implementers? Who is affected?
- **Where?** Where is the solution to be located? Where will the organization be after this is accomplished?

8.2.2 TYPES OF IMPLEMENTATION.

A new solution that does not replace an old solution can proceed along a straightforward timeline of implementation. A solution that replaces one already in place, however, must take into account the deactivation of the old solution. There are several methods for replacing one solution with another:

- **Cutover.** With a cutover implementation, the old solution is stopped completely and the new solution started immediately afterwards. The advantages of a cutover are that it is fast, and it preserves resources (extra staffing is not needed to maintain the old solution while beginning the new one). The disadvantages are that it may not be possible to return to the old solution easily if the new solution does not work, and that there is no direct comparison between the two solutions. For simple solutions, cutover is fine; for complex ones, it can be inexpensive but risky.

♦ **Pilot.** A pilot implementation tests the solution in a small way (for example, on part of the company data, on a few acres of the farm, or with a few students) to determine how well the solution is going to work. If the pilot program works out as expected, it is then expanded to the entire problem area.

♦ **Parallel.** A parallel implementation starts up the new solution while the old one is still fully functioning. The two solutions are operated at the same time, and comparisons are made to see if the new solution is better. For example, a new type of fighter aircraft is built and flown while the old jets are still being built and maintained. If the new aircraft does not perform to expectations, the old ones serve as a safe fallback. Once the new solution is determined to be working as hoped, the old solution is then terminated.

♦ **Staggered.** A staggered implementation takes a complex solution and breaks it into components. One component of the new solution is implemented at a time while the remaining components of the old solution are continued. When the first component is working as desired, the next new component is implemented (and its corresponding old component stopped). This process continues until the new solution has completely replaced the old one.

Regardless of the type of implementation chosen for the new solution, the old method or solution should be ended (and made unavailable) at some point. Leaving it in place will tempt people to ignore or reject the new implementation.

8.2.3 IMPLEMENTATION TIMELINE.

Chapter 5, Section 5.4.2 discussed the desirability of creating time frames for implementing a solution, and indeed, time is at the heart of implementation. The science of project management (such as building a billion-dollar hotel) is structured around time goals. The point to be emphasized is that for almost all solutions, establishing multiple deadlines is the most effective way to implement them.

The use of multiple deadlines helps overcome a common tendency for people to delay working on a task until the deadline for completion nears. When the deadline looms, work increases exponentially, as the graph on the next page reveals. This phenomenon can be a problem when the work required is so vast that even with fever-pitch attention at the end, the goal may be unreachable.

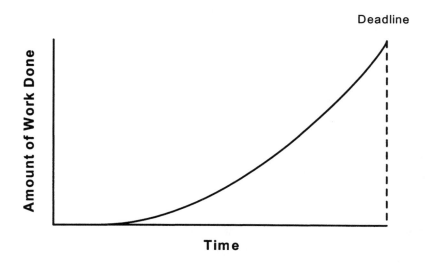

Representation of Work Done Under a Single Deadline

The solution is to create a series of intermediate deadlines, so that the solution implementers will be motivated at regular intervals to work toward the deadline. Multiple deadlines create multiple spurts of activity, as the graph below shows.

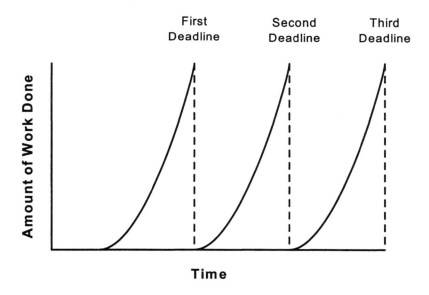

Representation of Work Done Under Multiple Deadlines

8.2.4 MAKE ADJUSTMENTS OR CHANGES AS NEEDED.

Practically every solution needs some modification in the process of being put into effect. Blueprints are changed, scripts are rewritten, formulas are adjusted. Remember that an implementation plan is a guideline, not a straightjacket. Remain flexible as the implementation proceeds, and be prepared to make necessary modifications.

QUESTIONS FOR REVIEW AND DISCUSSION.

1. The concept of acceptance for a solution refers to
    A. a solution that is technically competent to solve the problem.
    B. the emotional reception a solution receives by those affected.
    C. the correspondence between a solution and the identified goals.

2. You are designing a new roller coaster for an amusement park. Explain why the limits of technology are not the ultimate constraint in how "wild" the ride can be.

3. The Key of Wisdom tells us that "Fear of loss is more powerful than hope of gain" in part because
    A. both gain and loss are uncertain.
    B. the loss seems certain while the gain seems uncertain.
    C. the gain seems certain while the loss is uncertain.
    D. both gain and loss are certain, but no one likes losing anything.

4. Ways to reduce the FUD factor include all **except**
    A. offering reasons for the change.
    B. showing how the change harmonizes with stated goals.
    C. reassuring people that fear is all in their minds.
    D. discussing personal benefits to those affected.
    E. putting the change in context and including a time frame.

5. The expected negative consequences of a change should
    A. never be revealed in advance.
    B. always be revealed in advance.

6. In your opinion, of the four types of implementation (*cutover, pilot, parallel, staggered*), which would be best for re-landscaping an existing desert golf course with a new type of tree? Explain your choice.

7. In order to implement a large-scale solution involving much work,
    A. multiple intermediate deadlines should be established.
    B. a single deadline should be focused on with a "countdown to D-Day" constantly reminding people of it.

Chapter 9
❖
The Problem-Solving Cycle 6
Evaluating the Solution

Assessment should be designed to *improve* performance, not
just monitor it.
—Grant P. Wiggins

Error ceases to be error when it is corrected.
—Mahatma Gandhi

This chapter covers the final step in the problem-solving cycle, Evaluating the Solution.

```
The Problem-Solving Cycle
Exploring the Problem
Establishing Goals
Generating Ideas
Choosing the Solution
Implementing the Solution
➔ Evaluating the Solution ⬅
```

This chapter emphasizes the following aspects of solution evaluation:
- The degree of success of the solution should always be determined.
- If necessary, adjustments or changes should be made to the solution to assure its maximum effectiveness.
- If the solution did not work, another solution should be implemented.
- The original problem should also be examined for changes.

9.1 ANALYZE THE IMPLEMENTATION.

Often the weakest link in the creative problem-solving process is at the end, where the solution is implemented and then essentially forgotten. Neglecting to examine whether the solution actually worked is a common problem. Rather than rushing off after implementation, take some time to attend to the solution and to analyze the outcome.

9.1.1 WAS THE SOLUTION FULLY AND ACCURATELY IMPLEMENTED?

The first question to be asked in any implementation analysis should be whether the solution-as-designed was actually put into effect. Solutions are sometimes tried and abandoned, met with obstacles and detoured, or faced with administrative changes that turn the solution into something quite different from its original design. In all these cases, criticizing the failure of the solution-as-designed would be unfair because it was never actually implemented.

> **Example 9.1.1.1**
> "Our plan to reduce shoplifting by using security tags on the clothing did not work. Shoplifting was reduced only marginally." "Was the plan fully implemented?" "Well, corporate asked for a cost reduction, so instead of tagging every item of clothing, each store received 200 tags to place randomly among the 4,000 items in the store." "No doubt the shoplifters were careful to take only items without tags."

If the solution was not implemented as intended, examine the causes to determine whether or not they are reasonable or necessary. If not, can the solution still be implemented?

9.1.2 DID THE SOLUTION WORK?

Taking into account the stated goals, the concept of acceptance (from Chapter 8, Section 8.1), and the type of solution designed (stop-it or mop-it, discussed in Chapter 7), did the solution work? Several related questions should be answered carefully as part of this analysis of efficacy:

- ◆ **How well was the problem solved?** Is the solution merely adequate or quite satisfying? Is the problem gone for the foreseeable future, or does the solution appear to be only a temporary remedy? Is this a *high-quality* solution? (See the box on the next page, "What Is Quality?" for more information.)
- ◆ **Was the problem solved completely or only partially?** If a complete solution was designed but only a partial solution resulted, what was the cause?
- ◆ **Do both the solution designers and those affected by the solution agree that the problem was solved?** The difference in perspective can be surprising. Surveys or interviews of all those involved in the solution should be part of the evaluation process.

9.1.3 WERE THERE UNANTICIPATED, UNDESIRABLE CONSEQUENCES?

In Chapter 7, Section 7.5.1, we noted that solutions are sometimes the cause of problems. Consequence analysis is intended to help avoid the creation of problems through the implementation of a solution, but not all consequences are foreseeable. Part of implementation analysis, then, should be to identify any unanticipated negatives resulting from the solution, together with the generation of some ideas to mitigate those negative effects.

While you are in the process of noting unanticipated consequences, it might be useful to note unexpected benefits as well.

What Is Quality?

Quality is a measure of excellence. Specifically, quality refers to how well something measures up to its ideal state. The ideal state is defined by a set of controlling criteria (goals, characteristics, or standards), often set not only by the designers of the item but by its users, and based on the design's intended function. The closer the result comes to reaching the ideal state, the higher the quality. The more challenging the criteria, the greater potential for excellence, as the following Key of Wisdom tells us:

A better match to better criteria yields better quality.

Example criteria for a quality car would include reliability, durability, and comfort. (Note that not just physical things but also ideas, systems, procedures, policies, and so forth can all be evaluated for quality this way.)

9.2 DETERMINE NEEDED CHANGES.

An expression used in business seminars to encourage executives to be active leaders of change is, "Ready, fire, aim!" (See Peters & Waterman, 1982, Chapter 5.) The expression makes little sense if you are thinking of a single-bullet approach to problem solving. However, if you think of a solution as a machine gun, or less violently, a fire hose, then the expression makes great sense. The point is that if the solution does not work as originally implemented, you need not give up on solving the problem. There are several actions available to you: You can change the aim of the solution to hit the target.

9.2.1 DOES THE SOLUTION NEED TO BE ADJUSTED?

Just as it was recommended to make adjustments to the solution activities during implementation (Chapter 8, Section 8.2.4), an after-implementation analysis may reveal further alterations required to complete the solution (that is, to meet the desired goals fully).

Example 9.2.1.1

A man needs a new job, so he reads a book on interviewing techniques. The book recommends that he "express confidence" at the interviews. After several interviews that do not result in a job offer, he overhears one of the human resources people refer to him as arrogant. For future interviews, he adjusts his display of confidence to a more appropriate level.

Many activities might be viewed as solution-path adjustments. Changing study habits to get higher scores on tests, rewriting essays to increase the clarity of their meaning, and even changing the setting on a vacuum cleaner to match the carpet thickness are all examples: The basic solution activity is correct, but it needs to be tweaked in order to solve the problem better.

9.2.2 DOES THE SOLUTION REQUIRE ADDITIONAL SOLUTION ACTIVITIES?

Evaluation may reveal that a chosen solution works partially but by itself cannot solve the problem. In this event, adding another solution activity to the solution path will often prove helpful. The solution suite may involve a separate solution activity for each of several aspects of the problem or redundant solution activities to address the problem as completely as possible.

Example 9.2.2.1

Problem: You cut your finger and do not want an infection. Solution: Put on a bandage with some antibiotic ointment. But that might not guarantee freedom from infection. Revised solution: Use triple antibiotic ointment, with three antibiotics in it. (The next time you pick up a tube of this ointment in the store, remark knowingly, "Ah, three solution activities on a single path." Impress your friends!)

Example 9.2.2.2

Problem: The company needs to communicate the policy prohibiting sales representatives from giving gifts over a $50 value to customers. Solution: Print an article in the company newsletter. Result: Some but not all sales representatives have received the message. Revised solution: Create redundant communication channels. Send memos or e-mails, have supervisors call meetings, put posters on the walls, make a video, send a letter to employees' homes, etc.

9.2.3 SHOULD THE SOLUTION BE REPLACED BY ANOTHER SOLUTION?

Occasionally, evaluation will reveal that a solution did not work and cannot be made to work. An entirely new solution must be implemented if the problem is to be solved. In a situation like this, you will be happy that you took the advice in Chapter 7, Section 7.6.3, about selecting a Plan B while in the process of choosing a primary solution. A backup plan is always a good idea.

Example 9.2.3.1

A professor noticed that two students who seemed to lack an understanding of the material nevertheless received near-perfect scores on the first test. Thinking that the students had obtained the test from a previous student, the professor wrote an entirely new test for the next unit and carefully locked both his office door and the outer department door. The solution did not work: The students again got near-perfect scores. The professor then tried an entirely different solution. He wrote two tests for the third unit—the real test and a fake test. He placed the fake test in his office, locked the doors, and took the real test home. Soon, the real test was given and graded. When it was returned, the two students were quite surprised to see that they had answered every question wrong, by using answers to the questions on the fake test. (The professor later discovered that one of the students worked for campus maintenance and had a master key.)

9.3 REVIEW THE PROBLEM ENVIRONMENT.

Large-scale solutions, such as building a new automobile factory to respond to increased demand, require substantial time to implement. Part of the risk of large-scale projects like this is that the problem environment may change during implementation. Reviewing the problem should therefore be as much a part of the evaluation as examining the solution.

9.3.1 HAS THE PROBLEM SITUATION CHANGED?

Failure of a solution to solve a problem may result from a change in the problem rather than from an inadequacy of the solution to solve the originally targeted problem. Whenever a solution is not a success, then, the implementation evaluation should include another look at the problem itself.

Example 9.3.1.1

A few years ago, computer antivirus software detected the presence of a virus by matching a piece of the virus code to a pattern stored in the antivirus program's database. Matching code is still a common technique today, and users are encouraged to download new pattern files regularly. However, the problem situation changed when virus writers became more sophisticated. They encrypted the virus code, gave it stealth behavior (the ability to hide from detection) and provided the means for the virus to change itself into many forms (polymorphism). In these cases, the virus may no longer have a unique pattern of code that can be detected. As a result, while antivirus software continues to look for known viral patterns, it now must also include detection schemes that look for suspicious activities (such as an attempt to erase a protected area on a disk drive) that might reveal the presence of a virus.

Occasionally, moving-target problems like the one described above may appear to have disappeared. However, they may have merely become invisible or entered a dormant phase. Forgetting about problems that disappear this way is risky, as this Key of Wisdom reminds us:

⚷ Problems that go away by themselves often come back by themselves.

9.3.2 SHOULD THE PROBLEM-SOLVING CYCLE BE REVISITED?

The problem-solving cycle is called a cycle because the problem solver can circle back through it at any time, in a repeating process. Moreover, the problem solver can reach back to any step in the process and does not need to start at the first step. Depending on the circumstances, the solver may return to step four to select another solution, to step two to establish some new goals (in light of a new problem situation), or to step three to generate some new ideas.

The problem-solving cycle is a tool to be used in the way you find most effective; it is a guide to help you solve problems, not an inflexible framework.

QUESTIONS FOR REVIEW AND DISCUSSION.

1. The determination that a problem has been solved should be agreed upon by
   A. the solution designers.
   B. all groups affected by the solution.
   (C) both A and B.

2. Which would **not** be a way to improve the quality of a solution?
   A. Develop better controlling criteria.
   B. Match the solution more closely with the original criteria.
   C. Develop more challenging criteria and a closer match to them.
   (D) Think of quality in abstract terms, not as a product of intended function.

3. Identify the type of change for each of the following: *solution path adjustment, additional solution path activity,* or *replacement solution.*
   (a) A manufacturer of insulated coffee mugs markets them through late-night infomercials. The mugs do not sell well, so the manufacturer decides instead to sell the mugs by direct mail, using a mailing list of camping equipment buyers. replacement solution
   (b) A store installs lower wattage bulbs in the display areas to lower electricity usage and costs. When the reduction is less than expected, the store turns off its waterfall pumps, also. additional solution path activity
   (c) A homeowner bothered by ants puts baited traps around the house at 30-foot intervals. When the ant activity is reduced only a little, the homeowner puts the traps at 10-foot intervals. solution path adjustment

4. Twenty years ago, Lush Hills Estates installed storm drains from its streets to the ocean. The drains did not pollute the ocean then, but they do now.
   A. This solution probably did not work to begin with.
   B. The problem may have been solved at first but may now have changed.
   C. The solution failed because the problem most likely cannot be solved.

Appendix A

❖

Creative Thinking Activities

At the heart of creative thinking is a flexible mind. These activities will help you develop that flexibility by putting you in the habit of thinking of ideas and alternatives.

A.1 USES FOR.

With this technique, choose an ordinary object and think of possible uses for it other than the uses for which it was intended. The more uses you think of, the more creative they become. Often, the first few ideas for uses will be more ordinary than later ones. For each item, think of at least 10 alternate uses.

Example A.1.1
What are some uses for the paper dots that result from punching holes in making three-ring binder paper?
- ◆ Fill diapers with them.
- ◆ Dry your hands in a pile of them, instead of paper towels.
- ◆ Mix them with paint and spray on the walls for texture and decoration.
- ◆ Put them in the walls of a house for insulation.
- ◆ Use them as kitty litter.
- ◆ Pour them around goods as packing material.
- ◆ Press them into blocks for firewood.
- ◆ Sprinkle them from overhead as artificial snow.
- ◆ Throw them as party confetti.
- ◆ Use them as filler in jackets for winter insulation.
- ◆ Fill a room three feet deep as a paper ocean for kids.
- ◆ Stuff mattresses with them.
- ◆ Put them in food as a high-fiber additive.
- ◆ Soak them in fire retardant and blow them out of hoses onto fires.
- ◆ Pour them on oil spills to soak up the oil.
- ◆ Drop them from the blimp at a football game to celebrate a touchdown.

For the purposes of this exercise, the uses do not have to be extremely practical (mattress stuffing would not really work well), but they should be possible. The goal at this point is to flex your imagination. If you think of a possible use, write it down without criticizing or rejecting it.

ACTIVITY A.1.1

Choose one of the items below and think of at least 10 new uses for it. Think of uses for a single item and for many units of the item. For example, what uses are there for one Popsicle® stick and for many Popsicle sticks? Describe each use in a sentence or two and include drawings if you wish.

a cardboard box	a spoon
a roll of adding machine paper	a candle
a Popsicle stick	a towel
a sheet of paper	an inner tube
a marble	a steak knife

ACTIVITY A.1.2

Choose one of the items below and think of at least 10 new uses for it. Think of uses for a single item and for many units of the item. For example, what uses are there for one paper clip and for many paper clips? Describe each use in a sentence or two and include drawings if you wish.

a broken rubber band	an out-of-round metal ball
an empty soda pop bottle	an outdated CD-ROM disc
a paper clip	an old shirt
dried coffee grounds	beach sand
a broken television set	a broom

ACTIVITY A.1.3

You have been hired by the Breaking Dawn manufacturing company to write an advertising brochure for its new product, the Versa Tarp. The product is an ordinary eight- by ten-foot plastic tarp similar to that found in hardware stores and home centers everywhere. The tarp features reinforced edges and grommets for attaching cords or ropes. In the brochure, the company wants you to list as many good, practical uses for this tarp as you can, to show just how versatile it is. List at least 10 practical uses, with explanations or drawings if needed. (For example, "To use the tarp as a camping tent, run a rope between two trees and place the tarp over it. Tie down the edges of the tarp to form a triangular tent.")

A.2 IMPROVEMENTS TO.

This activity involves choosing an item and thinking about ways to improve it. What can be added or changed to make the item better? As with Uses For in A.1, the object is to develop your creative thinking flexibility rather than invent something ruthlessly practical (though you might do that, too).

Example A.2.1
How can a coffee cup be improved?
- ◆ Provide multiple handles.

- Put an antiskid coating on the bottom.
- Build in a heater to keep the coffee hot.
- Add a thermometer or temperature-revealing liquid crystal display.
- Provide many more shapes (triangular, oval, hexagonal).
- Have the restaurant version signal the waitress when it is low.
- Print jokes or other information on the side.
- Make the disposable ones easier to recycle or even reuse.
- Put a tea bag holding compartment under the base.
- Add a timer to indicate when the tea is brewed to taste.

ACTIVITY A.2.1

Choose one of the following items and think of at least 10 ways it can be improved. Describe each improvement in a sentence or two and add any needed explanations or drawings.

a pencil	the postal system
dating	paper
museums	a dog house
a textbook	spelling rules
a kitchen	a desk

ACTIVITY A.2.2

Choose one of the following items and think of at least 10 ways it can be improved. Describe each improvement in a sentence or two and add any needed explanations or drawings.

a daily newspaper	a flashlight
a bicycle	a telephone book
fast-food hamburgers	a public library
a Web site of your choice	student motivation
a vacation to the mountains	airline travel

A.3 WHAT IS IT?

For this activity, choose an abstract shape and imagine what different things it might be. This is an exercise in stretching your imagination and changing your approach to the shape. Is the item very large, very small, seen sideways or from the top?

This activity shows the benefits of incubation, which is the process of allowing your subconscious mind to work on a problem while you do something else (such as another task or even sleeping). Often the best ideas will come over a period of time. Think of as many things as you can and then put the activity aside for a while. Later in the day, return to it and see what else comes to mind.

Example A.3.1

What could this shape be? It might be a pyramid seen from the side (a very large object), a road sign (a smaller object), or a pill (even smaller), or a printer's bullet point. Or, it could be three runways on an airfield. Perhaps it's a caveman's first wheel (in need of improvement, of course). Other possibilities might be a teepee, the gable of a house, a delta-wing fighter plane, a pump impeller, a tunnel entrance, a snack cracker, a fulcrum for a scale.

ACTIVITY A.3.1

Imagine what possible things this shape could be. Think of at least 10 different items, and describe each one in a clear phrase or sentence. Remember to view it as large and small and mentally to walk around it, over it, and under it.

ACTIVITY A.3.2

Imagine what possible things this shape could be. Think of at least 10 different items, and describe each one in a clear phrase or sentence. Remember to view it as large and small and mentally to walk around it, over it, and under it.

ACTIVITY A.3.3

Imagine what possible things this shape could be. Think of at least 10 different items, and describe each one in a clear phrase or sentence. Remember to view it as large and small and mentally to walk around it, over it, and under it.

A.4 WRITING CAPTIONS.

For this activity, locate an illustration that shows at least two people in any situation. Now create at least 10 different captions for the illustration. A caption can be either a title for the scene or the words one or more of the people in the photograph are speaking. The captions need not be funny, but humor is a great stimulus to creativity—and makes this activity much more fun.

Example A.4.1

The photograph shows a man having just opened the door of a closet in which a skeleton is hanging. The man is looking at the skeleton.

- ♦ "Jane, I think your diet has gone too far."
- ♦ "I'm sorry, sir, but we are reduced to a skeleton crew today."
- ♦ "Ted, don't try to fool me. I can see right through you."

- ◆ "Marge, I've got a bone to pick with you."
- ◆ Room service in some hotels is very slow.
- ◆ "Hmm. The hip bone really is connected to the thigh bone."
- ◆ "But doctor, you said to take everything off."
- ◆ "Hey, nice calcium!"
- ◆ "Okay, *now* I'm sure there's nothing up your sleeve. Let me see you do that magic trick again."
- ◆ "Whoa! That's the hottest spa I've ever been in!"
- ◆ When chiropractors dream.
- ◆ Now you can buy X-ray glasses that really work.
- ◆ "After that meeting, I feel like I've been eaten alive."

ACTIVITY A.4.1

Locate a magazine advertisement with two or more people and write 10 captions for it. Many advertisements lend themselves to satirical or otherwise amusing comments. What are those models really thinking? What is the real title of the advertisement?

ACTIVITY A.4.2

Locate a cartoon, cut off or white out the cartoonist's gag, and write 10 captions for the cartoon.

A.5 WHAT IFFING.

This activity stimulates your creative mind by asking you to change reality in some imaginative way and then trace the logical consequences—good, bad, and indifferent—that would result. The exercise requires both creative and critical faculties to perform well. However, no evaluative judgment of the idea itself is involved.

Example A.5.1

What if rocks were soft?
- ◆ We could put big ones in our houses like pillows to lean on in the living room. (Beanbag chairs would not sell anymore.)
- ◆ We could use them like "medicine balls" to toss to each other for exercise.
- ◆ We could line roads with piles of rocks to keep cars from damage when control was lost on dangerous corners.
- ◆ We could jump off high buildings onto rock piles.
- ◆ Crushed rock pits could be used to jump into by athletes.
- ◆ On the other hand, rock-grinding wheels would not work anymore.
- ◆ Concrete, made of rock, would be soft.
- ◆ A cinderblock cell would be a padded cell.

After you get used to the process, try the activities with new realities that might actually occur. An additional goal here is for you to learn not to be threatened by new ideas, even if they appear to have negative consequences at first. (A bad idea can often lead to a good idea.) Relax and remember that the ideas are not being advocated but are merely being used as a thinking exercise. (When some people were asked, "What's good about a plan to charge a dollar a mile to drive a car?" they got angry, stopped thinking, and yelled, "Nothing!")

Example A.5.2

What if automobiles were all owned by the government and everybody had a key and could use any car that was handy?

- Parking-lot size could be reduced.
- There would probably be more car pooling with strangers.
- If the government also repaired the cars, there would be no personal pride in ownership, and many would be in minimal condition.
- On sunny days, cars would be plentiful, but on rainy days, you might get stuck at the shopping center.
- Cars that broke down would be abandoned.
- You could not lock things in your car.
- You would never know if the car you drove to a location (like the movie theater at night) would be there when you got out.
- People would leave trash in the car when they were through driving.

ACTIVITY A.5.1

Choose one of the questions below and then describe at least 10 reasonable and logical consequences that could follow. Include good, bad, and neutral consequences.

What if anyone could set up as a doctor?
What if each home could run the television only one hour a day?
What if a citizen could serve only one term in one office during a lifetime?
What if exams and grades were abolished in college?
What if our pets could talk?

ACTIVITY A.5.2

Choose one of the questions below and then describe at least 10 reasonable and logical consequences that would follow. Include good, bad, and neutral consequences.

What if gasoline cost $25 a gallon?
What if we never had to sleep?
What if we could read other people's minds (and they could read ours)?
What if all marriages were cancelled by the state every three years?
What if everybody looked almost exactly alike?

Appendix B

Brainstorming Activities

Following are some topics for use in personal or group brainstorming. See Chapter 6, Section 6.4, for the brainstorming guidelines.

B.1 NEW NAMES.

For the following activities, think of at least 10 possible new names for the item described. The names may consist of either one or two words. One-word names may be newly created words (as in "Nasadrane"). Two-word names must be created from two actual words (as in "Majestic Sunset").

If you want to find out whether a name is already a trademark, you can go to the U. S. government's trademark search service (TESS) at www.uspto.gov.

ACTIVITY B.1.1

Choose one of the following and create at least 10 new names for it. Follow the directions above.

> a red rose with white tips
> a light green paint color
> a blueberry-flavored soft drink
> a new perfume for women 18-29 years old
> a wheat cereal for kids, with multicolored pieces in plump circular shapes

ACTIVITY B.1.2

Create a name for a company that now makes food items (bread, cake mix, cereal, soup), household products (light bulbs, telephones, dishwashing detergent), and automotive products for manufacturers (mufflers and shock absorbers). Suggest 10 possible names and then choose one that appears to be the best. In a few sentences, explain why this is the best choice.

B.2 EMPTY THE GLASS.

A glass of water is placed on a card table. Think of at least 10 ways to empty the glass without touching it or knocking it over.

B.3 NO COUNTERFEITS.

Think of at least 10 ways to prevent the counterfeiting of concert tickets. Then choose the best one(s) and explain your choice(s).

Appendix C
❖
Problem-Solving Activities

C.1 ANALYZING A SOLUTION.

Use this activity to help you develop the habit of analyzing your world as a collection of solutions to problems. In a bookstore, for example, shelves and tables provide solutions to the problem of how to present books for sale. A chair solves the problem of how to sit or rest. A pill solves the problem of how to dispense a fixed dose of aspirin.

For this activity, observe your environment and locate three solutions. The solutions can be any kind (for example, technical or social). For each one, answer the following in about a sentence each.

- ♦ What was the problem?
- ♦ How was it solved?
- ♦ How well was it solved?
- ♦ What other solutions can you think of?

C.2 A FAMILIAR PROBLEM.

Choose a problem from your own past experience or observation. Next, in a sentence or two each, answer the following questions.

- ♦ What was the problem?
- ♦ How was it addressed at the time?
- ♦ What has been the result? (Was it solved? How well?)
- ♦ What other approach might have solved it?

C.3 MANY SOLUTIONS.

For this activity, follow these steps:

- ♦ Choose one of the problems below.
- ♦ Name at least five ways the problem has been solved, based on your experience and observation.
- ♦ State which of the solutions appear to be better and why.

a fence to keep animals out
sealing up leftover food
presenting visual aids during a lecture
a way to hold sheets of paper together

packaging juice for sale
a way to hold shoes on feet
how to choose who will go first
covering the floor in a house

References

Ackoff, R. (1978). *The art of problem solving: Accompanied by Ackoff's fables.* New York: John Wiley.

Adams, J. (1986). *The care and feeding of ideas: A guide to encouraging creativity.* Reading, MA: Addison-Wesley.

Davis, G. (1986). *Creativity is forever* (2nd ed.). Dubuque, Iowa: Kendall/Hunt.

de Bono, E. (1970/1973). *Lateral thinking: Creativity step by step.* New York: Harper & Row.

Koberg, D. & Bagnall, J. (1981). *The revised all new universal traveler.* Los Altos, CA: William Kaufmann.

Mayer, R. (1992). *Thinking, problem solving, cognition* (2nd ed.). New York: W. H. Freeman.

National Transportation Safety Board. (n.d.). DCA90MA019. Retrieved April 12, 2001, from the World Wide Web: http://www.ntsb.gov/ntsb/brief.asp?ev_id+20001212X22401&key+1

Osborn, A. (1963). *Applied Imagination: Principles and procedures of creative problem-solving* (3rd ed.). New York: Scribner's.

Peters, T. & Waterman, R. (1982/1984). *In search of excellence: Lessons from America's best-run companies.* New York: Warner Books.

Weisberg, R. (1993). *Creativity: Beyond the myth of genius.* New York: W.H. Freeman.

Index

Abstract representation 39
acceptance 83-87
alternative explanations 43
alternative ideas 11
analytic techniques 60-63
associative techniques 57-60
assumption articulation 40-43
attribute analysis 60-61

Becoming someone else 68
brainstorming 5, 14, 65-67

Causal reduction 31
causation 29-35
chain of causation 31
change 2, 27, 86-87
changing direction 4-5, 8
close analogy 59
consequence analysis 76-79
consequences 92
constraints 84-85
constructive discontent 19
continuous quality
    improvement 7
contributory cause 30
corporate values 49
correlation and cause 31
creative questions 63
creative thinking 1-6
criteria 49
critical thinking 5
cum hoc, ergo propter hoc 31
curiosity 19, 24
cutover 87-88

Deliberately chosen problem 26
denial 28
direct consequences 77
direct transfer 58
disconfirming evidence 44-45

Eliminate-it solution 73
emotional constraints 84-85
entrenched solutions 15
ethical values 49
evolution 6-8
externally caused problem 26

Fallacies of causation 31
fear of failure 14
fishbone diagram 33
flexibility 24
forced analogy 60
functional fixity 16-17

Goal state 2, 27, 75-76

goals 27, 47

Hot-potato problems 28
hypotheses 43

Ideal goals 51-52
imagination 3, 23, 67
implementation design 87-90
implementation timeline 88-89
indirect consequences 77
inflexibility 15-19
instant judgment 17

Journalistic six 38, 87
judgment 14

Kinds of causes 30
knowledge filter 44

Learned helplessness 12
legal values 49
long-term consequences 78

Matrix of causation 35
mental metamorphosis 68
mental playfulness 23
mental practice 67
mop-it solutions 73-74
moving-target problem 95
multidirectional why 63
multiple causation 33
multiple viewpoints 43

Necessary assumptions 41
necessary cause 30
negative attitudes 11

Openness to change 24
optimism 20, 24
ownership of problems 27

Parallel implementation 88
parallel why 63
path fixation 9
perseverance 12, 22, 24
personal values 50
physical consequences 77-78
physical constraints 84
pilot implementation 88
plan B 79, 94
points of attack 45
post hoc, ergo propter hoc 31
practical goals 52-54
preconceived solution 38
prejudice 16
premature closure 28
prepositions 65
prevent-it solution 72-73
problem 2, 25-27, 37-40

problem environment 95
problems as solutions 21
proximate cause 30
psychological blocks 18, 84
public solution 63

Quality 92-93
questioning attitude 19

Ranking solutions 79
reapplication 6
redirect-it solution 74
reduce-it solution 73
regulatory values 49
religious values 49
remote analogy 59
reversal 61-63
revolution 8
risk taking 24
rival hypotheses 43, 44-45
role playing 67

Serial why 64
short-term consequences 78
social consequences 77-78
solution 71-75
solution evaluation 91-93
solution path 9, 48, 75-76
solution path activity 75-76
solution suite 75-76
solutions as problems 76-77
specific targets 53
staggered implementation 88
stepping stones 18, 67
stop-gap solutions 75
stop-it solutions 72-73
storytelling 3
subproblems 27
sufficient cause 30
suspend judgment 22
synthesis 8

Timetable 53
tolerate-it solution 74
treat-it solution 74

Unstructured problems v, 3
using criticism 80

Values 49-51

Why tree 64